A CHARTWELL-BRATT STUDENT TEXT

D1741580

The Intensive C Course

by Mick Farmer

Department of Computer Science
Birkbeck College, University of London

Chartwell-Bratt   Studentlitteratur

For Melanie

"Wouldst thou" -- so the helmsman answered, --
"Learn the secret of the C?
Only those who brave its dangers
Comprehend its mystery!"†

---

†With apologies to Longfellow [1].

Chartwell-Bratt (Publishing and Training) Limited,
ISBN 0-86238-114-2

Printed in Sweden by Studentlitteratur, Lund

ISBN 91-44-26511-5   2 3 4 5 6 7 8 9 10 | 1991 90 89 88 87

Preface

This book teaches you how to write good C programs. It illustrates the principles of good programming style and sound design. It also demonstrates that C is easy to learn and fun to use. The language described is the current draft standard [2] which is about to be approved. It includes many new features which aid program reliability and portability.

The introduction begins with a brief review of the language's history and contains a bibliography of other useful books relating to C. Chapter 1 contains an overview of the language and its component features. After reading this chapter, existing programmers will be able to write C code. Chapter 2 describes expressions, with an emphasis on examples. After reading this chapter, novice programmers will be able to write C programs. Chapter 3 describes declarations. Chapter 4 describes the different statements and control structures. Chapter 5 describes functions, the major building blocks of the language, and programs. Chapter 6 describes array structures, pointers, and pointer arithmetic. Chapter 7 describes the remaining aggregates, namely structures, unions, and bit-fields. Chapter 8 covers the preprocessor. Chapter 9 describes the standard library functions. These functions form the interface between a program and its environment. Chapter 10 deals with additional tools like *lint*, *adb*, and *prof* which assist the C programmer. Each chapter contains numerous examples of working C programs.

There are appendices describing the syntax of C, the working environment of a C program, the ASCII character set, and the UNIX† system calls.

---

†UNIX is a Trademark of AT&T Bell Laboratories.

Acknowledgements

Firstly, my thanks to Dilys Gane for her editorial comments and to Philip Riebold for proof reading the drafts. Secondly, my thanks to our data preparation department, Linda Bailey, Sheila Hailey, and Barbara Whitmore, for patiently preparing the index. Finally, a thank you to all the students who have endured my lectures and, by their comments and criticism, have helped shaped this book.

The text was prepared, and the examples tested, on my UNIX system (Version 7). Of all the operating systems I have used, UNIX is the only one that is a help in getting a job done rather than an obstacle to be overcome. The world-wide acceptance of UNIX, and with it the C language, indicates that I am not alone in feeling this way.

All the programs described in this book are available in machine-readable form from the author.

Mick Farmer

Contents

List of Figures

Introduction

C is a general-purpose programming language featuring economy of expression, good control flow, modern data structures, and a rich set of operators. It is powerful because it includes natural control structures and data types, allowing their uses to be as unrestricted as possible. The language is also easy to learn.

The C language [3] is the result of several years of development. Many of its important ideas stem from an older language, BCPL [4], developed by Martin Richards at Cambridge University. BCPL is a typeless language that supports only one object, the machine word. All operations are defined for machine words and storage is allocated on this basis. BCPL compilers were used in the 1960s for writing operating systems [5]. From BCPL, Ken Thompson at Bell Labs. in 1970 developed another language, B [6], for the UNIX operating system on the DEC PDP-11. B and BCPL differ mainly in their syntax but are semantically very close. The machine model of BCPL and B is simple and consistent but it is inefficient on modern machines. One problem with B was discovered when UNIX was implemented on the PDP-11. The word addressing of B meant that accessing bytes (within words) was inconvenient. This, and other problems with B, led the UNIX team to design a new language which is now known as C†.

The major advance provided by C was its typing structure. Each type determines how much storage an object of that type requires and how it is to be interpreted. By the time that C was created (1972) languages such as Algol 68 [7] and Pascal [8] were encouraging (enforcing?) strong typing. The C compiler, the UNIX operating system and all UNIX application programs are written in C. However, the language is not tied to any particular hardware or operating system. C compilers run on a wide range of machines from small microcomputers, such as the Sinclair Spectrum [9], to

†It was originally called NB (Not B).

large super-computers, such as the Cray 2 [10]. To complete the picture, personal computer-based C cross-compilers are available for the latest microcontrollers [11].

There will soon be an International Standards Organisation (ISO) standard for C specifying the syntax and semantics of the language together with the standard library definitions that work with C [2]. This book describes that standard. The various standards committees keep as a major goal to preserve the *Spirit of C*. The Rationale which accompanies the new standard summarises the Spirit of C as follows ([12], p.3)

- Trust the programmer.

- Don't prevent the programmer from doing what needs to be done.

- Keep the language small and simple.

- Provide only one way to do an operation.

- Make it fast, even if it is not guaranteed to be portable.

This last proverb will provide food for thought throughout this book.

Bibliography

The *de facto* standard for the C language is currently *The C Programming Language* by Brian Kernighan and Dennis Ritchie [3]. This book is not an introductory text. The examples are mainly complete programs, rather than isolated fragments.

The American National Standards Committee have issued a preliminary draft describing the C programming language [2]. This document is currently being circulated for comment in Europe by ISO and in Great Britain by the British Standards Institute (BSI).

A Book on C by Al Kelley and Ira Pohl [13] contains dozens of working C programs, most with a numeric flavour.

C for Programmers by Leendert Ammeraal [14] demonstrates, through examples, that C programming is enjoyable.

Existing Pascal programmers may find *From Pascal to C* by Douglas Brown [15] a useful additional text.

Comparative Languages by Jon Malone [16] is a good text for collectors of programming languages, or those who want to compare C with other procedural languages.

Existing UNIX users coming to C for the first time should read *The UNIX System* by Steve Bourne [17] because he shows how C fits into the overall system. It is also a very good practical guide to the UNIX operating system for all classes of user.

There is a growing folk history about UNIX and C. A fascinating retrospective by Dennis Ritchie and others can be found in the July-August 1978 issue of the Bell System Technical Journal devoted to the UNIX operating system [18].

Chapter 1
All at C

1.1 Introduction

While C is not a large, specialised, high-level language, it offers the advantages of high-level programming and an efficiency approaching that of assembly language. Its absence of restrictions and its generality make C a convenient language, more effective than many which are supposedly more powerful.† This is partly because C is terse. However, it is not difficult to learn, as shown by the numerous examples.

C is not without criticism. Only with the current standard [2] has the question of strong typing been addressed, and this only relates to function parameters. There is no array bound checking. The compiler can re-order the evaluation of expressions. It heavily overloads certain symbols. However, it is an elegant language.

The examples in this book assume a modern interactive environment. This implies that input comes from the terminal's keyboard and that output is displayed on the terminal's screen. All of the programs make this assumption. On UNIX it is so easy to re-direct input from a file and to re-direct output into a file that this is often the normal mode of working. Now read on.

---

†C has fewer keywords (reserved words) than Pascal and it is more powerful.

Example 1.1

Reading and writing programs is the best way to learn a programming language. This program illustrates some of the features of C. From the standard input the program reads an integer value which represents the radius of a circle. It then prints on the standard output the area of the circle. It repeats this sequence until the input is exhausted (end-of-file).

```
 1  /*circle.c*/
 2  #include <stdio.h>
 3  #define PI       3.14159265
 4  int radius;
 5  int main(void)
 6  {
 7      while(scanf("%d", &radius) != EOF) {
 8          double area = PI*radius*radius;
 9          printf("%f\n", area);
10      }
11  }
```

The section headings below refer to line numbers in the program listing above.

(1) Anything written between /* and */ is a comment and is ignored by the compiler. All the program listings in this book start with a comment which gives the name of the file which contains the program (see Section 1.7). There are no other comments! This omission is a terribly bad practice ([19], pp.108-111).

(2) This is a preprocessor control line which specifies that the standard input/output library should be included with this program (see Section 8.2).

(3) This is a preprocessor control line which defines the identifier *PI* to be the character string "3.14159265". The use of symbolic constants in a program makes it more readable. In addition, it is easy to change the constant later (see Section 8.3).

(4) This is a declaration. *Int* is a keyword which informs the compiler that *radius* is an integer variable (see Section 3.3).

(5) Every program contains a function called *main()* where execution begins (see Section 5.4). The keyword *void* indicates that the function is defined with no parameters.

(6)   The braces on lines 6 and 11 surround the body of a function (see Section 5.2).

(7)   The *while* statement is repeatedly executed until the expression within parentheses becomes false (see Section 4.4.1). The expression is testing the value returned by *scanf()* against the symbolic constant *EOF* (defined in <stdio.h>). *Scanf()* also reads an integer value into the variable *radius* (see Section 9.12.3). The string "%d" is the input conversion specifier. The braces on lines 7 and 10 surround a *compound statement* (see Section 4.2).

(8)   This is a declaration with initialisation. *Double* is a keyword which informs the compiler that *area* is a double-precision variable. It is initialised to the value of the expression (see Chapter 2).

(9)   This statement contains a call to the function *printf()* which prints the value of *area* as a floating-point number (see Section 9.12.3).

1.2 Keywords

The lower-case identifiers given in Figure 1.1 are reserved for use as keywords.

auto	break	case	char
const	continue	default	do
double	else	enum	extern
float	for	goto	if
int	long	register	return
short	signed	sizeof	static
struct	switch	typedef	union
unsigned	void	volatile	while

Figure 1.1 -- Keywords

Some older compilers may not include *const*, *signed*, and *volatile* as keywords.

1.3 Identifiers

An identifier is a sequence of letters (lower-case

letters and upper-case letters), digits, and underscores
(_). The first character must be a letter or underscore.
It is a C tradition to use lower-case for variable names and
upper-case for symbolic constants. There is no specific
limit on the maximum length of an identifier. The number of
significant characters in an identifier is variable. For an
internal identifier, Kernighan & Ritchie [3] state that the
first eight characters are significant. However the proposed C standard [2] states that at least 31 characters are
significant. *External identifiers*, used by linkers or
loaders, are more restrictive, with six characters (possibly
ignoring alphabetic case) being the norm.† Obviously these
limits are implementation-dependent. Some valid identifiers
are

```
        n               /*single-character*/
        abc             /*multiple-character*/
        the_big_one     /*descriptive?*/
        Fortran77       /*mixed letters and digits*/
        QUERY           /*symbolic constant?*/
        _               /*bizarre*/
```

but the following are invalid

```
        complete#hash       /*character # is invalid*/
        10_green_bottles    /*digit can't be first*/
        COBOL-74            /*additive expression*/
```

1.4 Constants

There are many types of constant. Each type is
uniquely determined by its representation. Floating-point
constants contain a decimal point or exponent part, integer
constants do not. Character constants are contained in
single-quotes, string constants in double-quotes. Identifiers declared as enumeration constants are discussed
separately in Section 3.4.2. Examples of the other types
are given below.

---

†This is a painful recognition the C must coexist with
other languages and older assemblers and linkers for
years to come.

1.4.1 Floating-point Constants

A floating-point constant is a decimal number, option-ally in scientific notation, containing either a decimal point, an exponent part, or both. An unsuffixed floating-point constant is of type *double*. The suffixes f and F denote type *float*, the suffixes l and L denote type *long double*. Some valid floating-point constants are

```
0.0             /*zero*/
12.             /*better to write 12.0*/
.34             /*better to write 0.34*/
12.34           /*is of type double*/
12.34F          /*is of type float*/
12.34L          /*is of type long double*/
123e4           /*1230000.0*/
12.34e-5        /*0.0001234*/
12.e3           /*12000.0*/
.12e3           /*120.0*/
```

but the following are invalid

```
1234    /*integer constant*/
1,234.5 /*integer and double in a comma expression*/
-12.34  /*double constant expression*/
```

1.4.2 Integer Constants

An integer constant has no decimal point or exponent part. An optional prefix (0 for octal, 0x or 0X for hexade-cimal) determines its base. An optional suffix (l or L for *long*, u or U for *unsigned*) determines its type. The letters a to f, or A to F, represent the hexadecimal values ten to fifteen. Some valid integer constants are

```
0               /*zero*/
0L              /*long zero*/
1234            /*decimal constant*/
0567            /*octal constant*/
0x89a           /*hexadecimal constant*/
32768           /*int or long constant*/
123456789L      /*long constant*/
0123U           /*unsigned (octal) constant*/
456UL           /*unsigned long constant*/
```

but the following are invalid

```
-123      /*integer constant expression*/
123.0     /*double constant*/
1,234     /*two integers in a comma expression*/
```

The digit *1* and the letter *l* look similar, so it is advisable to use only the letter *L* as the suffix for a *long* constant. A constant integer that does not fit into an *int* will automatically be promoted to *long*, and then to *unsigned long* before an error is announced. Similar rules for the *unsigned* flavours of *int* also apply. An implementation using 2-byte *int*s and 4-byte *long*s will treat the number *32768* as a *long*. It is easy to overlook the zero prefix for octal constants. 123 is different from 0123.†

1.4.3 Character Constants

A character constant is a single character enclosed in single-quotes. It is of type *char*. Its value is implementation-dependent. In the ASCII character set (see Appendix B) the character 'x' has the value octal 0170, or decimal 120. Certain non-graphic characters are represented by an escape sequence (within single-quotes)

```
\a        /*alert (bell)*/
\\        /*backslash*/
\b        /*backspace*/
\r        /*carriage return*/
\"        /*double-quote*/
\f        /*form feed*/
\xhhh     /*hexadecimal integer (up to 3 digits)*/
\t        /*horizontal tab*/
\n        /*newline*/
\ooo      /*octal integer (up to 3 digits)*/
\?        /*question mark*/
\'        /*single-quote*/
\v        /*vertical tab*/
```

The double-quote and question mark are represented by themselves or by the specified escape sequences. This set is taken from the proposed standard for C [2]. However, some current implementations may not include this complete set. Note that the motion control escape sequences avoid

---

†Octal 0123 is equal to decimal 83.

any western alphabet assumption that printing advances left
to right and from top to bottom. The result of an escape
sequence other than those given above is implementation-
dependent.

1.4.4 String Constants

A string constant consists of zero or more characters
enclosed in double-quotes. The compiler automatically
appends the *NUL* character '\0' to the end of the string.
Its type is "array of *char*". Non-graphic characters are
represented by the escape sequences given in Section 1.4.3
above as in


```
"\033G4Please speak after the tone\a\033G0"
```

which displays the embedded message and alert in inverse-
video on a Televideo 925 VDU [20]. A long string constant
can be continued across multiple lines by using a
backslash-newline combination,† or by "pasting" two strings
together. These two examples are equivalent


```
        lower = "abcdefghijklm\
nopqrstuvwxyz";

        lower = "abcdefghijklm"
                "nopqrstuvwxyz";
```


The first example requires the string which follows the
backslash to start at the beginning of a line (otherwise
white space is inserted). The second example is preferable
for preserving program layout and style.

Example 1.2

There is a traditional first program in C books, which
has been *internationalised* (see Assignment 9.3). It prints
variations on the string "Hello, world" on the standard output. Note the explicit newline character; *printf*() only
prints what it is told to.

---

†The backslash character, \, at the end of a line.

```
1 /*hello.c*/
2 #include <stdio.h>
3 int main(void)
4 {
5     printf("Hello, world\n");
6     printf("Bonjour, le monde\n");
7     printf("Ola, mundo\n");
8     printf("Buon giorno, mondo\n");
9 }
```

Be aware of the difference between a character constant and a string constant containing a single character. 'x' is a single character and different from "x" which is a character string consisting of two characters, the letter x followed by *NUL*.

1.5 Operators

An operator specifies an action involving one or more operands which results in a value. Figure 1.2 gives the full list.

```
| [     ]     (          )     .      -> |
| ++    --    &          *     +      -  |
| ~     !     sizeof     /     %      << |
| >>    <     >          <=    >=     == |
| !=    ^     |          &&    ||     ?  |
| :     =     *=         /=    %=     += |
| -=    <<=   >>=        &=    ^=     |= |
| ,     #     ##                         |
```

Figure 1.2 -- Operators

The effect of these operators is described in detail in Chapter 2, with the exception of # and ## which can only occur in preprocessor directives and are described in Chapter 8. This overloading of characters to form operators means that a mistyped or missing character yields unexpected (and often undetected!) results. Some common examples are

```
a = b    /*instead of a == b*/
a > b    /*instead of a >> b*/
a =! b   /*instead of a != b*/
a != b   /*instead of a |= b*/
a & b    /*instead of a && b*/
a | b    /*instead of a || b*/
```

Note that these are all valid expressions which yield a value and a type.

1.6 Punctuation

Punctuation symbols are syntactically and semantically significant but do not specify an action resulting in a value. Figure 1.3 gives the full list.

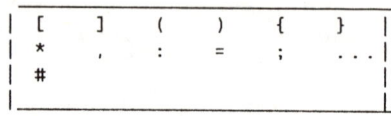

Figure 1.3 -- Punctuation Characters

The punctuator # can only occur in preprocessor directives (see Chapter 8). A comment consists of the characters /* and everything else† up to and including the characters */ as in the following example

```
/****************************
* This is a neat comment *
* put carefully in a box *
****************************/
```

White space (blanks, comments, newlines, and tabs) is ignored except where it is required to separate adjacent identifiers and keywords.

C was originally based on the ASCII character set which, unfortunately, is not a subset of all other commonly used character sets. For example, it is widespread practice in Europe to use parts of the ASCII collating sequence for special national characters. To allow all C characters to be represented, additional *trigraph* sequences have been defined (see Section B.2).

---

†Including newlines and other occurrences of /*

1.7 Running a C Program

The detailed method of running a program depends on the
system that you are using. This book assumes you are using
UNIX. Other operating systems provide the same facilities
in a different form.

(1)   Create a text (source) file whose name ends in .c, for
      example

                    ed myprog.c

      where *ed* is the name of a text editor.

(2)   Compile the program using a C compiler, for example

                    cc myprog.c

      which will create an executable file *a.out* if there are
      no compile-time errors. If errors are reported, repeat
      from step (1) by modifying the program.

(3)   It may be necessary to explicitly link† the program
      with other object modules or libraries in order to
      create an executable version. On UNIX in the simple
      case this is performed behind the scenes in the previ-
      ous step with the compiler invoking the linker itself.
      For example, a command like

                    ld myprog.o -lm

      will combine the specified object file with the maths
      library into the executable file *a.out*. This technique
      is especially useful for building a large program from
      smaller, separately compiled, pieces ([21], pp.8-10).

(4)   Execute the program. The command

                    a.out

      achieves this on UNIX. If run-time errors occur, again
      repeat from step (1) by modifying the program.

      Tools that help programmers locate errors are described

---
†This may be called loading or consolidating on other
systems.

in Chapter 10.   These include *lint* for   detecting   compile-
time errors and *adb* for detecting run-time errors.

1.8 The NODDY Software Corporation

        Most of the assignments in this book involve   writing
and   running   programs.   The   employee   records   at   NODDY
Software Corporation provide test data for some of the examples and some of the assignments.   These data are in a text
file, one employee record per line.   See Figure 1.4 below.


```
 157 Jones,  Tim             12000   199 01/02/1940 03/04/1960
1110 Smith,  Paul             6000    33 05/06/1952 07/08/1973
  35 Evans,  Michael          5000    32 09/10/1952 11/12/1974
 129 Thomas, Tom             10000   199 13/01/1941 14/02/1962
  13 Edwards, Peter           9000   199 15/03/1928 16/04/1958
 215 Collins, Joanne          7000    10 17/05/1950 18/06/1971
  55 James,  Mary            12000   199 19/07/1920 20/08/1969
  26 Thompson, Bob           13000   199 21/09/1930 22/10/1970
  98 Williams, Judy           9000   199 23/11/1935 24/12/1969
  32 Smythe, Carol            9050   199 25/01/1929 26/02/1967
  33 Hayes,  Evelyn          10100   199 27/03/1931 28/04/1963
 199 Bullock, J.D.           27000     0 29/05/1920 30/06/1920
4901 Bailey, Chas M.          8377    32 31/07/1956 01/08/1975
 843 Schmidt, Herman         11204    26 02/09/1936 03/10/1956
2398 Wallace, Maggie J.       7880    26 04/11/1940 05/12/1959
1639 Choy,   Wanda           11160    55 06/01/1947 07/02/1970
5119 Ferro,  Tony            13621    55 08/03/1939 09/04/1963
  37 Raveen, Lemont          11985    26 10/05/1950 11/06/1974
5219 Williams, Bruce         13374    33 12/07/1944 13/08/1959
1523 Zugnoni, Arthur A.      19868   129 14/09/1928 15/10/1949
 430 Brunet, Paul C.         17674   129 16/11/1938 17/12/1959
 994 Iwano,  Masahiro        15641   129 18/01/1944 19/02/1970
1330 Onstad, Richard          8779    13 20/03/1952 21/04/1971
  10 Ross,   Stanley         15908   199 22/05/1927 23/06/1945
  11 Ross,   Stuart          12067   994 24/07/1931 25/08/1932
```

        Figure 1.4 -- The NODDY Software Corporation

The fields are

•   Employee number in columns 1 to 4.

•   Employee name in columns 6 to 25.

•   Employee salary in columns 27 to 31.

- Employee's manager (number) in columns 33 to 36.

- Employee's birthday (dd/mm/yyyy) in columns 38 to 47.

- Employee's starting date with the corporation (dd/mm/yyyy) in columns 49 to 58.

Assignment 1.1

Say whether the following statements are true or false. You may not be able to answer them all now, if not come back and repeat them after you have finished the book.

(a) C was designed by Brian Kernighan and Dennis Ritchie.

(b) The language was called C because that letter comes between the initial letters of Brian and Dennis.

(c) C can only be run under the UNIX operating system.

(d) A statement in C is just an expression with a semicolon on the end.

(e) *Boolean* is a defined data type.

(f) *Character* is a defined data type.

(g) *Const* is a defined data type.

(h) "*xfab*" is a character constant.

(i) '*xfab*' is a character constant.

(j) "*con*" "*catenate*" is a string constant.

(k) *What? John: QED* is an expression.

(l) *1,234,567.89* is a floating-point constant.

Assignment 1.2

Modify the program given in Example 1.1 so that it computes the *circumference* of the circle. Comment on the changes that you make.

Assignment 1.3

Writing programs is probably the best way to learn a language, especially during an intensive course like this.

(a) Decide where to run your programs and make friends with the operating system.

(b) Decide which editor to use and get used to its features and quirks. Remember that over 90% of your time in front of a terminal is spent editing text files. Screen editors are generally easier to use than line editors. However, there may be difficulties if you are using a networked terminal.

(c) Decide which C compiler to use by compiling some short programs. If you are using UNIX the portable C compiler, *pcc*, may also be available. In particular, learn to interpret the compiler's diagnostic messages.

(d) Learn how to run your compiled programs. Investigate what mechanisms are available for reading input from a file instead of the keyboard and for writing output to a file instead of the VDU screen. On some unfriendly systems this may mean modifying the program.

(e) Learn to find your way round the manuals. Take notes that you can refer to later. Make friends with your system's guru (it is easier if you buy them a drink).

Chapter 2
Expressions

2.1 Introduction

An *expression* is a sequence of operators and operands that specifies how to compute a value. The order of evaluation of an expression is unspecified except for the rules given below.

(1) The rules of *precedence* as indicated by the syntax (see Appendix A). For example, this implies that a + b * c is parsed as a + (b * c) and that a * b + c is parsed as (a * b) + c.

(2) The rules of *associativity* as specified later in this chapter. For example, this implies that a = b = c is parsed as a = (b = c) and that a == b == c is parsed as (a == b) == c.

Furthermore, an expression which contains one or more occurrences of the same commutative and associative binary operator (e.g. +, *, &, etc.) may be evaluated in any order provided that the types of the operands, or of the result, are not changed. For example, if a is of type *long* and b and c are of type *int*, the expression a + (b + c) must be evaluated according to the parentheses. However the expression 2 * (b * c) could be evaluated in any order, such as b * (2 * c).

C uses a bewildering number of operators involving sixteen precedence levels and both left to right and right to left associativity. Note that parentheses (used in function calls) and brackets (used for array subscripting) are classified as operators. Unary operators such as +, -, *, etc. have a higher precedence than their binary versions. Figure 2.1 lists all the operators in order from the highest to the lowest precedence.

Operators	Associativity
[] () . -> ++ --	left to right
++ -- * & + - ! ~ sizeof	right to left
(type)	right to left
* / %	left to right
+ -	left to right
<< >>	left to right
< <= > >=	left to right
== !=	left to right
&	left to right
^	left to right
|	left to right
&&	left to right
||	left to right
?:	right to left
= += -= *= /= %= >>= <<= &= ^= |=	right to left
,	left to right

Figure 2.1 -- Operators and Associativity

Examples of these operators are given later in this chapter. The operators # and ## can only occur in preprocessing directives and are therefore described in Chapter 8.

2.2 Arithmetic Conversions

An expression is evaluated by reference to some simple rules. Conversions may take place irrespective of whether the operands are of the same or of different types. Consider the arithmetic expression

a op b

If necessary, the following four conversions can be applied to the operands. Bit-fields (see Section 7.4) are also converted to the correct flavour of *int*.

(1) *char* is converted to *int*.

(2) *unsigned char* is converted to *unsigned*.

(3) *short* is converted to *int*.

(4) *unsigned short* is converted to *unsigned*.

Now, if the expression is of mixed type, the operand of the "lower" type is promoted to the type of the "higher" operand according to the hierarchy

        long double
        double
        float
        unsigned long
        long
        unsigned
        int

Note that floating-point arithmetic <u>can</u> be performed in single- or double-precision. Older compilers use double-precision throughout. Even if the expression is not of mixed type, automatic conversions take place. In the expression

'a' - 'b'

both character constants are converted to *int*, using rule (1) above, and the type of the result is *int*. Also, under certain conditions, actual parameters in a function call may be automatically converted (see Section 5.3).

2.3 Lvalue Expressions

An *lvalue* is an expression which refers to an object and which can be used to change the value of that object. Some operators yield lvalues. The sections below describe the operators and indicate whether lvalues are expected as operands or whether the result is an lvalue. For example, after the declarations

```
    int i;              /*integer variable*/
    char c[3];          /*array of three characters*/
```

i is an lvalue of type *int* and *c[2]* is an lvalue of type *char*. Note that *c* is not an lvalue.† However, see Section 6.3 for a minor complication.

2.4 Primary Expressions

An identifier is a primary expression only if it has been suitably declared (see Section 3.4). Function names and array identifiers are not lvalues.

A constant is a primary expression but not an lvalue. Its type depends on its representation, as discussed previously in Section 1.4.

A parenthesised expression is a primary expression whose value and type are the same as the expression without parentheses. It may or may not be an lvalue.

```
    mick_farmer            /*identifier*/
    123.456e78             /*double constant*/
    12345                  /*integer constant*/
    'x'                    /*character constant*/
    "Birkbeck College"     /*string constant*/
    (jack & jill)          /*parenthesised expression*/
```

---

†It is of array type (see Section 6.2).

2.5 Postfixed operators

The postfixed operators associate left to right and have the highest precedence. A primary expression is a postfixed expression as are the following examples

```
table[index]     /*array subscript*/
index[table]     /*yes, it's possible*/
bubble(a, MAX)   /*function call*/
my.name          /*field selection*/
your->salary     /*same as (*your).salary*/
count++          /*postfix increment*/
lives--          /*postfix decrement*/
```

A postfix expression of the form $E1[E2]$ is a subscript reference to an array object. It is defined to be identical to the unary expression $(*(E1+(E2)))$. This is because of the conversion rules that apply to the binary + operator (see Section 2.9). Array subscripting is covered in more detail in Chapter 6.

A postfix expression of the form $E1(E2, ...)$ is a function call. The parentheses are mandatory, even if there are no actual parameters. A function may return a value of any type of object except array or function. The result is not an lvalue. Functions are covered in more detail in Chapter 5.

A postfix expression of the form $E1.I1$ or $E1->I1$ is a reference to a member of a structure or union. $E1$ must be of structure or union type and $I1$ must be a named member of that type. The result may be an lvalue referring to the named member, $I1$, of the structure or union. For example, $f().x$ is a valid postfix expression but is not an lvalue. Structures and unions are covered in more detail in Chapter 7.

In a postfix expression of the form $E1++$ the expression $E1$ must be an lvalue. The value of the result is the value of $E1$. It is not an lvalue. After the result is noted, the lvalue is incremented by adding one (of the appropriate type) to it. If b is an *int* with the value 3, then after the assignment expression

```
a = b++
```

a has the value 3 and b has the value 4.

The postfix operator -- is analogous to the postfix

operator ++ except that the lvalue is decremented after the value is noted.

2.6 Unary Operators

The unary operators associate right to left. A post-fixed expression is a unary expression as are the following examples

```
++girl_friends   /*prefix increment*/
--boy_friends    /*prefix decrement*/
*zoom            /*indirection*/
&postcode        /*pointer to*/
+nothing         /*unary plus*/
-balance         /*unary minus*/
!truth           /*logical negation*/
~bits            /*one's complement*/
sizeof table     /*size of object in bytes*/
sizeof(int)      /*size of type in bytes*/
```

In a prefix expression of the form ++*E1* the expression *E1* must be an lvalue. The lvalue is incremented and the value of the result is this new value which is not an lvalue. If *b* is an *int* with the value 3, then after the expression

$$a = ++b$$

both *a* and *b* have the value 4. The prefix operator -- is analogous to the prefix operator ++ except that the lvalue is decremented before the value is noted.

The unary * operation denotes indirection. If the operand points to a function, the result is an expression by which the function can be called (see Section 3.4). If the operand points to an object, the result is an lvalue desig-nating that object.

The result of the unary & (meaning address of) operator is a pointer to the object designated by its operand. If *E1* is an lvalue, then *&E1* is an lvalue equal to *E1*. The unary & operator cannot be applied to a *register* object (see Sec-tion 3.2.3) or a bit-field object (see Section 7.4).

The expression +*E1* is equivalent to the expression (*0*+*E1*). The operand must be arithmetic. The result is not an lvalue. This operator can be used to force evaluation of sub-expressions. In the expression

$$a + +(b + c)$$

the operands a and $(b + c)$ are evaluated separately.

The expression $-E1$ is equivalent to the expression $(0-E1)$. The operand must be arithmetic. The result is not an lvalue.

The expression $!E1$ is equivalent to the equality expression $(0==E1)$. This logical negation gives interesting results. If an expression is non-zero the result is zero, otherwise the result is one. This means that the equality expression

$$a == !!a$$

is true only when a has the value zero or the value one. The result is not an lvalue.

The result of the ~ operator is the bitwise complement of its operand. The operand must be integral. The result is not an lvalue.

The result of the *sizeof* operator is the size, in bytes, of its operand which may be an expression or a parenthesised type name. The result is not an lvalue.

Example 2.1

This program prints the sizes of the basic data types in C. The values are in bytes.

```
 1  /*sizeof.c*/
 2  #include <stdio.h>
 3  int main(void)
 4  {
 5      printf("char\t%d\n", sizeof(char));
 6      printf("unsigned char\t%d\n",
 7          sizeof(unsigned char));
 8      printf("short\t%d\n", sizeof(short));
 9      printf("unsigned short\t%d\n",
10          sizeof(unsigned short));
11      printf("int\t%d\n", sizeof(int));
12      printf("unsigned\t%d\n", sizeof(unsigned));
13      printf("long\t%d\n", sizeof(long));
14      printf("unsigned long\t%d\n",
```

```
15                sizeof(unsigned long));
16         printf("float\t%d\n", sizeof(float));
17         printf("double\t%d\n", sizeof(double));
18         printf("long double\t%d\n", sizeof(long double));
19 }
```

2.7 Cast Operators

The cast operators associate right to left. A
parenthesised type name in front of an expression is called
a *cast*. It converts the value of the expression to the
named type. The operator only applies to scalar types. In
the cast

$$(\ T1 \ ) \ E1$$

the expression *E1* is first evaluated and then its value is
converted to type *T1*. The result is not an lvalue.

Example 2.2

This program for converting Celsius to Fahrenheit
illustrates the use of a *cast*. The parenthesised expression
on line 11 is of type *double* and is explicitly converted by
the use of a cast to *int* before the assignment to
fahrenheit.

```
 1 /*ctof1.c*/
 2 #include <stdio.h>
 3 #define LOW     0
 4 #define HIGH    100
 5 #define MULBY   1.8
 6 #define ADDIN   32.5
 7 int main(void)
 8 {
 9      int celsius;
10      for(celsius = LOW; celsius <= HIGH; celsius++) {
11           int fahrenheit = (int)(celsius*MULBY+ADDIN);
12           printf("%3d\t%3d\n", celsius, fahrenheit);
13      }
14 }
```

2.8 Multiplicative Operators

The multiplicative operators *, /, and % associate left
to right. Each of the operands must be arithmetic and,
additionally, the operands of % must be integral.

```
a * b    /*multiplication*/
a / b    /*division (quotient)*/
a % b    /*division (remainder)*/
```

When positive integers are divided the result of the /
operator is the largest integer less than the true quotient
and the result of the % operator is positive. When either
operand is negative the results are implementation-
dependent. For integers a and b the logical expression

```
(b == 0) || ((a / b) * b + a % b == a)
```

is always true (see Section 2.12 and Section 2.17). The
parentheses around the equality expressions are not necessary, but aid readability and understanding.

Example 2.3

Choose any positive integer and call it *n*. If *n* is
even, divide it by two. If *n* is odd, multiply it by three
and add one. This yields a new value for *n*. Numbers in
this sequence are known as *hailstone numbers* because the
sequence resembles the trajectory of a hailstone through a
storm cloud, rising in updrafts and then falling under its
own weight [22]. Do the numbers tend to grow larger or
smaller? Does every sequence terminate by reaching one?

This program does not answer the question. It only
generates the sequences. However, it does illustrate the
multiplicative operators in action.

```
1 /*hailstone.c*/
2 #include <stdio.h>
3 int main(void)
4 {
5      int n;
6      scanf("%d", &n);
7      while(n > 1) {
8          if(n%2 == 0)
9              n = n/2;
```

```
10              else
11                  n = 3*n+1;
12              printf("%d\n", n);
13          }
14 }
```

2.9 Additive Operators

The additive operators + and - associate left to right. There are various combinations of valid operand types.

(1) *E1* + *E2*. Both operands may be arithmetic.

(2) *E1* + *E2*. One operand may be a pointer to an object and the other operand may be an integral expression. In this case the integral value is first multiplied by the size of the object pointed to. The result is a pointer of the same type as the original pointer (see Section 6.3).

(3) *E1* - *E2*. Both operands may be arithmetic.

(4) *E1* - *E2*. *E1* may be a pointer to an object and *E2* may be an integral expression. See (2) above.

(5) *E1* - *E2*. Both operands may be pointers to objects of the same type. In this case the difference is divided by the size of the object pointed to (see Section 6.3). The result is of integral type *ptrdiff_t* (see Section 9.11).

2.10 Bitwise Shift Operators

The shift operators << and >> associate left to right. The result of the shift expression

$$E1 << E2$$

is the (bit pattern) value of *E1* shifted left by *E2* bit positions with zero filling from the right. The result of the shift expression

$$E1 >> E2$$

is the (bit pattern) value of *E1* shifted right by *E2* bit positions. If the expression *E1* is of *unsigned* type the right shift is logical (zero filling from the left). Otherwise it may be logical or arithmetic (sign bit filling from the left) depending on the implementation.

Example 2.4

This example computes the number of bits in an *unsigned* integer by shifting right an initial pattern of all binary ones until the result is zero. Note that the compound assignment expression

w >>= 1

is equivalent to, and more elegant than, the simple assignment expression

w = w >> 1

The constant expression used as an initialiser on line 6 yields an implementation-independent pattern of all ones.

```
 1 /*wordlength.c*/
 2 #include <stdio.h>
 3 int main(void)
 4 {
 5     int n = 1;
 6     unsigned w = ~0;
 7     while((w >>= 1) > 0)
 8         n++;
 9     printf("Wordlength is %d\n", n);
10 }
```

2.11 Relational Operators

The relational operators < (less than), <= (less than or equal), > (greater than), and >= (greater than or equal) associate left to right. The value of the result is zero if the relation is false and one if the relation is true. The type of the result is always *int*.

(1)   Both operands may be arithmetic.

(2)   Both operands may be pointers to objects of the same
      type. In this case the value of the result depends on
      the relative locations of the objects (see Section
      6.3).

      The order of evaluation can give interesting results.
The relational expression

                    a <= b <= c

is not interpretated as in mathematics.   It is evaluated,
according to the syntax, as

                    (a <= b) <= c

which means that if *a* is less than or equal to *b* then one is
compared with *c* otherwise zero is compared with *c*.

2.12 Equality Operators

      The equality operators == (equal to) and != (not equal
to) associate left to right. The value of the result is
zero if the equality is false and one if it is true. The
type of the result is always *int*.

(1)   Both operands may be arithmetic.

(2)   Both operands may be pointers to objects of the same
      type.

(3)   One operand may be a pointer to an object and the other
      operand may be *NULL*, the null pointer.

      The result of the equality expression

                    a == b == c

is true only when *a* and *b* have the same value with *c* equal
to one or when *a* and *b* have different values with *c* equal to
zero.

2.13 Bitwise AND Operator

The bitwise AND operator & associates left to right. Each of the operands must be integral. The operands are treated as strings of binary digits and the result is implementation-dependent. This operator is primarily used for masking.

Example 2.5

This program reads its input as a stream of bytes. Each 8-bit byte has its two 4-bit nibbles ([23], p.324) exchanged. This is achieved by masking and shifting (on line 7).

```
1  /*nibble.c*/
2  #include <stdio.h>
3  int main(void)
4  {
5      char c;
6      while(scanf("%c", &c) != EOF) {
7          c = ((c&0xf)<<4)+((c&0xf0)>>4);
8          printf("%c", c);
9      }
10 }
```

2.14 Bitwise Exclusive OR Operator

The bitwise exclusive OR operator, ^, associates left to right. Each of the operands must be integral. The operands are treated as strings of binary digits and the result is implementation-dependent. Consider the following three statements which exchange the contents of two scalar variables without using a temporary location

$$x \mathrel{\hat{}}= y;$$
$$y \mathrel{\hat{}}= x;$$
$$x \mathrel{\hat{}}= y;$$

This technique is used in Example 8.1.

2.15 Bitwise Inclusive OR Operator

The bitwise inclusive OR operator, |, associates left to right and the operands must be integral. The operands are treated as strings of binary digits and the result is implementation-dependent. Line 7 in Example 2.5 above could be re-written using the bitwise inclusive OR operator as

```
c = c<<4&0xf0 | c>>4&0xf;
```

Note that parentheses round the operands are not necessary. However this expression is not easy to read, especially with strange precedences!

2.16 Logical AND Operator

The logical AND operator, &&, associates left to right. If both operands are non-zero the value of the result is one, otherwise the value of the result is zero. The type of the result is always *int*. The && operator guarantees left to right evaluation. If the value of the first operand is zero the second operand is not evaluated. In the following situation this is essential to prevent an invalid operation (contents of *NULL*)

```
if(p != NULL && p->next != NULL)
        p = p->next;
```

This operator is also demonstrated in Example 4.8.

2.17 Logical OR Operator

The logical OR operator, ||, associates left to right. If either of the operands is non-zero the value of the result is one, otherwise the value of the result is zero. The type of the result is always *int*. The || operator guarantees left to right evaluation. If the value of the first operand is non-zero the second operand is not evaluated.

Example 2.6

This program copies the standard input to the standard output, replacing each sequence of one or more blanks by a single blank. The bitwise inclusive OR operator <u>could</u> have been used, but it is less economical since it involves evaluation of both subexpressions every time.

```
1  /*blanks.c*/
2  #include <stdio.h>
3  #define BLANK   ' '
4  int main(void)
5  {
6      char c;
7      char prev = !BLANK;
8      while(scanf("%c", &c) != EOF) {
9          if(c != BLANK || prev != BLANK)
10             printf("%c", c);
11         prev = c;
12     }
13 }
```

2.18 Conditional Operator

Conditional expressions associate right to left. In the conditional expression

$$E1 \; ? \; E2 \; : \; E3$$

E1 is evaluated first. If its value is non-zero the result is the value of *E2*, otherwise the result is the value of *E3*. Thus either *E2* or *E3* is evaluated, but not both. The first operand must be a scalar. Both the second and third operands must be arithmetic or the same structure, union, or pointer type. If the second and third operands are arithmetic the usual arithmetic conversions are used to convert them to a common result type.

Example 2.7

This function is often coded as a macro (see Section 8.3.2).

```
1 /*max1.c*/
2 int max(int a, int b)
3 {
4         return(a > b ? a : b);
5 }
```

2.19 Assignment Operators

The assignment operators =, +=, -=, *=, /=, %=, >>=, <<=, &=, ^=, and |= associate right to left. Each assignment operator must have an lvalue as its left operand. An assignment expression has the type of the left operand and the value of the left operand after the assignment. The result is not an lvalue. If *a* and *c* are *ints*, *b* is a *float* with the value 5.6 and *d* is a *float* with the value 7.8, then after the statement

$$a = b + (c = d)$$

c has the value seven and *a* has the value 12. Note that an implicit conversion from *float* to *int* uses truncation.

A compound assignment expression

$$E1 \ op= \ E2$$

is equivalent to the simple assignment expression

$$E1 = E1 \ op \ (E2)$$

except that the lvalue of *E1* is only evaluated once. Note the parentheses round *E2*. are needed to ensure that expressions like

```
        a %= b + c        /*a = a%(b+c)*/
```

are evaluated correctly.

2.20 Comma Operator

The comma expression

E1 , E2

is evaluated left to right. *E1* is evaluated for its side effects and its value is discarded. The result is the type and value of *E2*. Most commas in programs do not represent comma operators. Commas are usually used to separate expressions in function argument lists or to separate common declarations. The comma expression in the following con-trived example must be parenthesised

```
this(is, (not = good, programming), style);
```

Comma expressions are commonly found in loops, as in the following example for counting the number of nodes in a singly-linked list

```
for(p = head, count = 0; p != NULL; p = p->next)
        count++;
```

Note that the expression *count++* could have been combined within the loop header as well!

Assignment 2.1

If *a* has the value 2, *b* has the value 3, and *c* has the value 4, what are the values of *a*, *b*, *c*, and the resultant expression in the following cases? Why are the parentheses necessary in case (c)?

(a)   a = b = c

(b)   a = b == c

(c)   a == (b = c)

(d)   a == b == c

(e)   a = b != c

(f)   a = b =! c

(g)   a != b != c

```
(h)    a =! b =! c

(i)    a + b++ + c

(j)    a + b + ++c

(k)    a + b + +c

(l)    a++ + b++ + c++
```

Assignment 2.2

Write a program that computes the average salary of the
employees at the NODDY Software Corporation (see Section
1.8). Input and output formatting is described in detail in
Section 9.12.3 but, for now, the function call

```
scanf("%*25c%d%*[^\n]%*c", &x)
```

will extract an employee's salary from a line of the standard input. Briefly, the format %*25c skips the first 25
characters (employee number and name), the format %d reads
an integer value (employee salary) into x, the format
%*[^\n] skips to the newline character at the end of the
line, and the format %*c skips the newline character. Note
also that the *address* of the variable is explicitly passed
to *scanf*(). Easy peasy!

Assignment 2.3

Languages such as Ada [24] and Pascal [25] put a great
deal of emphasis on the difference between expressions and
statements. Like C, languages such as Algol 68 [7], APL
[26], and POP-2 [27] do not make such a clear distinction.
They treat an assignment as a form of expression with a side
effect. Investigate this difference and present advantages
and disadvantages for the two approaches. Jon Malone's book
[16] would be a good starting point.

Chapter 3
Declarations

3.1 Introduction

A *declaration* specifies some or all of the attributes of an identifer. Empty declarations are invalid except for two special cases mentioned below. The declaration always specifies

(1) The type of the identifier, e.g. *char* or "array of *int*".

(2) The scope of the identifier, e.g. global or local to the current source file.

(3) The lifetime of the storage for that identifier, e.g. automatic on entry to the current function or static throughout the lifetime of the program.

A *definition* is a particular form of declaration which specifies

(4) The allocation of storage for the identifer, e.g. *int a[20]* or *char tictac[3][3]*.

(5) An initial value for the identifier, e.g. *int a = 123* or *double radius = circumference/(2*PI)*.

3.2 Storage Class Specifiers

The storage class specifiers are *auto*, *extern*, *register*, *static*, and *typedef*. Not more than one storage class specifier may be given in a declaration. If the specifier is omitted from a declaration, it defaults to *auto* inside a function and *extern* outside a function. Although not strictly a storage class specifier, *typedef* is important enough to have Section 3.6 to itself!

3.2.1 Auto

An object declared inside a function, or as a formal parameter, is by default automatic. The keyword *auto* is rarely used. In the example below both blocks are equivalent.

```
{                              {
        char c;                        auto char c;
        int i;                         auto int i;
        ...                            ...
}                              }
```

3.2.2 Extern

A declaration with storage class specifier *extern* indicates that an external declaration for the given identifier exists somewhere in the set of source files forming the complete program. The declaration

```
extern int getline();
```

specifies that *getline()* is a function returning an *int* which is defined somewhere else. In this case no information is provided about the formal parameters. The rule is that an external object can only be defined once, but references can be made to it, that is it can be declared many times. In the example below the variable *count* is defined in File 1 and declared in File 2.

```
int count;                          extern int count;
first()                             second()
{                                   {
      count = 1;                          count = 2;
      ...                                 ...
}                                   }
...                                 ...

   File 1                              File 2
```

When both files are compiled and linked together *count* refers to the same *int* variable.

3.2.3 Register

A declaration with storage class specifier *register* is an *auto* declaration with a recommendation to the compiler that the objects declared should be stored in fast-access registers. This means that the unary address-of (&) operator cannot be applied to such objects. The types of objects that can be stored in registers are implementation-dependent.

Example 3.1

This function converts an unsigned integer *n* into a string of hexadecimal digits in *s*. It is suggested that three variables should be stored in registers, thus making the object program shorter and faster. The declaration on line 7 implies that *h* is an *int*. *Reverse()* reverses the characters within a string and is defined in Example 6.2.

```
1  /*itoh.c*/
2  extern void reverse(char *s);
3  void itoh(register unsigned n, char *s)
4  {
5        register char *t = s;
6        do {
7              register h = n%16;
8              if(h <= 9)
9                    *t++ = h+'0';
10             else
11                   *t++ = h+'a'-10;
12       } while((n /= 16) != 0);
```

```
13        *t = '\0';
14        reverse(s);
15 }
```

3.2.4 Static

The storage class specifier *static* has two distinct uses.

(1) Its use permits a local object to retain its previous value when the block in which it was declared is reentered. This contrasts with an automatic variable, which loses its storage and therefore its value on block exit.

(2) External *static* objects provide a privacy mechanism. This is important for program modularity, especially when C programs are constructed from a number of separately compiled source files.

Example 3.2

This example illustrates how values are retained by *static* objects. Successive calls to *random*() generate a sequence of pseudo random numbers using a linear congruential method ([28], pp.9-10). The variable *seed* is initialised once only and retains its value between function calls.

```
 1 /*random.c*/
 2 #define INC    1
 3 #define MOD    16384
 4 #define MUL    125
 5 #define BEG    17
 6 long random(void)
 7 {
 8      static long seed = BEG;
 9      seed = (MUL*seed+INC)%MOD;
10      return(seed);
11 }
```

Example 3.3

Extern objects retain their values across block and function exit, so why use *static extern* objects? The reason is that such objects have a scope which is restricted to the current source file, that is, they are private to the file. In this example the variable *seed* and the function *random()* are not accessible from other source files. Successive calls to *normal()* generate a sequence of normalised pseudo random numbers in the range [0, 1).

```
 1 /*normal.c*/
 2 #define INC     1
 3 #define MOD     16384
 4 #define MUL     125
 5 #define BEG     17
 6 static long seed = BEG;
 7 static long random(void)
 8 {
 9      seed = (MUL*seed+INC)%MOD;
10      return(seed);
11 }
12 double normal(void)
13 {
14      return(random()/(double)MOD);
15 }
```

3.3 Type Specifiers

The type specifiers are *char*, *const*, *double*, *float*, *int*, *long*, *short*, *signed*, *unsigned*, *void*, and *volatile*. In addition a structure specifier, a union specifier, an enumeration specifier, and a typedef name behave as, or are treated as, type specifiers. The keywords *const*, *long*, *short*, *signed*, *unsigned*, and *volatile* may be used as adjectives or on their own. A missing type specifier defaults to *int*. Here are some examples

```
const            /*same as const int*/
long             /*same as long int*/
long float       /*same as double*/
short            /*same as short int*/
signed           /*same as signed int*/
unsigned         /*same as unsigned int*/
volatile         /*same as volatile int*/
```

The type modifier *const* indicates that the implementation can put *const* objects into read-only storage, and that the compiler is encouraged to diagnose obvious attempts to modify them.

There is a plethora of integer types involving their "signedness". There are four types of signed integer, called *signed char*, *short int*, *int*, and *long int*. A "plain" *char* may be *signed* or *unsigned*.† A "plain" *int* is always *signed*.

Similarly, there are four types of unsigned integers. A computation involving unsigned objects can never overflow because of the modulo arithmetic that is used.

Void is used to indicate that a function does not return a value, or in any context where the value of an expression is discarded. A function prototype with no arguments is written as *f(void)* to distinguish it from *f()* which means that while there may be arguments nothing is said about them. Functions are described in detail in Chapter 5.

The type modifier *volatile* is used for objects accessed in ways which are not obvious to the compiler, for example memory mapped I/O registers. The object declared as

        extern volatile const real_time_clock;

may be modifiable by hardware, but it cannot be assigned to, incremented, or decremented ([2], p.30).

Structures are described in Section 7.2, unions in Section 7.3, and typedefs in Section 3.6.

3.3.1 Enumeration Specifiers

The identifiers in an enumeration list are declared as constants of type *int*. An enumerator with = gives the identifier a value and subsequent constants are increased by one. If the first enumerator has no = the constant values begin at zero. The following example illustrates the supported values for the operator field in a File Transfer Protocol (FTP) parameter qualifier ([29], p.34). See also Example 7.2.

---

†As suggested by the architecture of the target environment.

```
enum operator {EQ = 2, LE, NE = 5, GE, ANY};
```

It is possible to write an empty *enum* declaration in order to introduce the constants, as in

```
enum {zero, one};
```

3.4 Declarators

Each declarator declares one identifier. The construction can be bizarre, but it is used consistently in both declarations and expressions. Parentheses can be used to specify precedence.

```
int i;          /*int*/
int *pi;        /*pointer to an int*/
int a[];        /*array of ints*/
int *ap[];      /*array of pointers to ints*/
int (*pa)[];    /*pointer to an array of ints*/
int f();        /*function returning an int*/
int *fp();      /*function returning a pointer to an int*/
int (*pf)();    /*pointer to a function returning an int*/
```

Taking the last example above it is possible to analyse the construction as follows

```
(*pf)() /*int*/
(*pf)   /*function returning an int*/
 *pf    /*parentheses alter precedence*/
  pf    /*pointer to a function returning an int*/
```

A pointer declarator may have a *const* modifier specifying the attributes of the pointer itself, as opposed to those of the base type. Consider these examples

```
const int *pci; /*pointer to constant int*/
int *const cpi; /*constant pointer to int*/
```

This is covered in more detail in Section 6.3.

Example 3.4

This example illustrates the declaration of a derived type, *struct date*, together with a variable of that type and a pointer to an object of that type. Structures are dealt with in more detail in Section 7.2.

```
1 /*date1.h*/
2 struct date {
3       short day;
4       short month;
5       short year;
6 } my_birthday = {10, 11, 1945},
7    *your_birthday = NULL;
```

3.5 Type Names

A *type name* is a declaration for an object of the specified type but without the identifier. This construction is occasionally required in a cast (see Section 2.6), as the argument to *sizeof* (see Section 2.5), or within a function prototype (see Section 5.2). Compare these examples with those in Section 3.4.

```
int              /*int*/
int *            /*pointer to an int*/
int [5]          /*array of five ints*/
int *[5]         /*array of five pointers to ints*/
int (*)[5]       /*pointer to an array of five ints*/
int ()           /*function returning an int*/
int *()          /*function returning a pointer to an int*/
int (*)()        /*pointer to a function returning an int*/
```

Some examples of these constructions are

```
int *malloc(SIZE)            /*void *malloc()*/
sizeof(char)                 /*always one*/
extern double sqrt(double)   /*function prototype*/
```

3.6 Type Definitions

A *typedef* declaration explicitly associates a type with an identifier, that is, it declares an identifier to be synonymous with the type. The construction looks like a declaration of the identifer. Some examples are

```
typedef double real;
typedef long integer;
typedef real poly[MAXDEGREE];
typedef char *string;
typedef enum {FALSE, TRUE} boolean;
typedef struct {real re, im;} complex;
```

These identifiers can be used as type names in subsequent declarations. For example

```
real x, y, z;      /*double x, y, z*/
integer i, j;      /*long int i, j*/
poly p;            /*double p[MAXDEGREE]*/
string s, t;       /*char *s, *t*/
boolean test;      /*enum {FALSE, TRUE} test*/
complex c;         /*struct {double re, im;} c*/
```

Correct use of *typedef*s means that implementation-dependent declarations (e.g. the size of an *int*) can be localised.† The source language is extended in a natural way and the programs are self-documenting. See Example 7.2.

Assignment 3.1

Write declarations for the following objects

(a) A static unsigned integer.

(b) An array of three double-precision constants.

(c) A pointer to a constant long double.

(d) A constant pointer to an array of ten characters.

---

†Frequently such declarations are collected together in a header file (see Section 8.2).

(e) A pointer to a function that returns a pointer to a function returning an integer.

(f) A union of an integer and a character.

(g) A structure containing an integer and two pointers to structures of the same type.

Assignment 3.2

Modify your program for Assignment 2.2 so that it additionally computes

(a) The minimum salary.

(b) The maximum salary.

(c) The median of the salaries.

Assignment 3.3

Declarations and definitions in C are a little eccentric. Languages such as Algol 68 [7] and Pascal [25] have very formal constructs for declaring objects. FORTRAN 77 [30] on the other hand, is less rigid and has some default rules which allow objects to be declared implicitly. Investigate how objects are declared in different languages and present advantages and disadvantages for the different approaches. Again Jon Malone's book [16] is a useful reference.

Chapter 4
Statements and Control Structures

4.1 Introduction

A simple statement is an expression followed by a semi-colon. A compound statement is a set of statements surrounded by braces. Consider these examples

```
a+b        /*expression*/
a+b;       /*statement*/
{a+b;}     /*statement*/
```

4.2 Compound Statements

A *compound statement*, or *block*, allows several statements to be grouped into a single statement. The word *block* is used to describe a compound statement containing some initial declarations.

Example 4.1

This function sorts the elements of an array into ascending order using a bubble sort ([31], pp.106-111). Blocks restrict the scope of names and make the programs more readable. In addition variables can be created only where they are needed. The fact that storage is released on block exit can be useful if memory is scarce.

```
1  /*bubble.c*/
2  bubble(int a[], int n)
3  {
4        int i;
5        for(i = n;  i > 0;  i--) {
6               int j;
7               for(j = 0;  j < i;  j++)
8                      if(a[j] > a[j+1]) {
9                             int k = a[j];
10                            a[j] = a[j+1];
11                            a[j+1] = k;
12                     }
13       }
14 }
```

In this example the scope of *i* is the block between lines 3
and 14, the scope of *j* is the block between lines 5 and 13,
and the scope of *k* is the block between lines 8 and 12.

4.3 Selection Statements

A selection statement chooses one from a set of statements.   The selection depends on the value of a controlling
expression. Only the *switch* statement is different from
similar constructs in other languages.

4.3.1 If Statement

In the first form of the conditional statement

                    if(E1) S1

the statement *S1* is executed only if the value of the
expression *E1* is non-zero. In the second form of the conditional statement

                    if(E1) S1 else S2

the statement *S1* is executed if the value of the expression
E1 is non-zero, otherwise statement *S2* is executed.

Example 4.2

This program counts the amount of whitespace on the standard input. Blanks, newlines, and tabs are counted separately. The body of the *while* loop demonstrates the use of a chain of *if* statements.

```
1  /*whitespace.c*/
2  #include <stdio.h>
3  #define BLANK     ' '
4  #define NEWLINE       '\n'
5  #define TAB       '\t'
6  int main(void)
7  {
8       char c;
9       int nb = 0;
10      int nl = 0;
11      int nt = 0;
12      while(scanf("%c", &c) != EOF) {
13          if(c == BLANK)
14              nb++;
15          else if(c == NEWLINE)
16              nl++;
17          else if(c == TAB)
18              nt++;
19      }
20      printf("Blanks\t%d\n", nb);
21      printf("Newlines\t%d\n", nl);
22      printf("Tabs\t%d\n", nt);
23  }
```

4.3.2 Switch Statement

The *switch* statement has the form

                    switch(E1) S1

causing control to be transferred to one of the statements in the switch body *S1*. The selection depends on the value of the controlling expression *E1*. This controlling expression can be of any integral type, even *unsigned long*. The switch body is usually a compound statement. It can contain statements labelled with one or more *case* prefixes of the form

```
                 case E2:
```

The expression *E2* must be a constant expression of the same integral type as the controlling expression. All constant expressions in the switch body must have different values. There may be no more than one *default* label in the switch body. If no *case* constant matches the controlling expression and there is no *default* label, the switch body is not executed.

The *case* and *default* prefixes are only labels, so *break* must be used to exit from the switch body (see Section 4.5.1). There is no provision for *case* ranges as exist in other languages, of the form *lo .. hi*.

Example 4.3

This program emulates a very cheap calculator. Expressions are input in infixed notation and there is no operator precedence. The program is written for an interactive environment so the input is not echoed.

```
 1 /*calculator1.c*/
 2 #include <stdio.h>
 3 int main(void)
 4 {
 5      float ac;
 6      char operator;
 7      while(scanf("%f%c", &ac, &operator) != EOF) {
 8          while(operator != '=') {
 9              float operand;
10              scanf("%f", &operand);
11              switch(operator) {
12              case '+':
13                  ac += operand;
14                  break;
15              case '-':
16                  ac -= operand;
17                  break;
18              case '*':
19                  ac *= operand;
20                  break;
21              case '/':
22                  ac /= operand;
23                  break;
24              default:
25                  printf("Invalid operand");
```

```
26                        break;
27                    }
28                    scanf("%c", &operator);
29                }
30                printf("%f\n", ac);
31        }
32 }
```

4.4 Iteration Statements

An iteration statement causes repeated execution of a statement called the *loop body*, the number of repetitions depends on the value of a controlling expression. The *for* statement is extremely general.

4.4.1 While Statement

In the *while* statement

$$while(\ E1 \ ) \ S1$$

the statement *S1* is repeatedly executed while the value of the expression *E1* is non-zero. The test takes place <u>before</u> the statement is executed. Thus the statement *S1* may never be executed.

Example 4.4

This program computes the value of the function

$$h(n) = 1 + 1/2 + 1/3 + \ldots + 1/n$$

using a *while* statement.

```
1 /*while.c*/
2 #include <stdio.h>
3 int main(void)
4 {
5        int n;
```

```
 6        float h = 0.0;
 7        scanf("%d", &n);
 8        printf("%d", n);
 9        while(n > 0) {
10             h += 1.0/n;
11             n--;
12        }
13        printf("\t%f\n", h);
14 }
```

4.4.2 Do Statement

In the *do* statement

                    do S1 while(E1)

the statement *S1* is repeatedly executed until the value of
the expression *E1* is zero. The test takes places <u>after</u> each
execution of the statement. Thus the statement *S1* is always
executed at least once.

Example 4.5

This program computes the value of the function $h(n)$
(see Example 4.4) using a *do* statement. This is a bad
choice of control structure for this problem because it cannot handle the situation when the input value is zero.†

```
 1 /*do.c*/
 2 #include <stdio.h>
 3 int main(void)
 4 {
 5        int n;
 6        float h = 0.0;
 7        scanf("%d", &n);
 8        printf("%d", n);
 9        do {
10             h += 1.0/n;
11             n--;
12        } while(n > 0);
```

---

†How does this example handle other non-positive input
values?

```
13          printf("\t%f\n", h);
14 }
```

Example 3.1 illustrated a situation where this control structure is required to ensure that the loop body is executed at least once.

4.4.3 For Statement

The *for* statement

$$for(\ E1 \ ; \ E2 \ ; \ E3 \ ) \ S1$$

is equivalent to

```
                    E1 ;
                    while( E2 ) {
                            S1 ;
                            E3
                    }
```

One or all of the expressions may be omitted. If *E2* is omitted the value is assumed to be one, i.e. the loop body is continually executed. A disadvantage of this very general control structure is that it does not facilitate optimisation of the loop. Heavily used control variables should be declared as *register* (see Section 3.2.3).

Example 4.6

This program computes the value of the function *h(n)* (see Example 4.4) using a *for* statement.

```
 1 /*for.c*/
 2 #include <stdio.h>
 3 int main(void)
 4 {
 5         int n, i;
 6         float h = 0.0;
 7         scanf("%d", &n);
 8         printf("%d", n);
 9         for(i = 1; i <= n; i++)
10                 h += 1.0/i;
```

```
11        printf("\t%f\n", h);
12 }
```

Example 4.7

A "perfect" number is a non-negative integer that equals the sum of its divisors (e.g. 1 + 2 + 3 == 6). This program reads integer values from the standard input and reports whether they are perfect or not. It demonstrates a combination of selection statements and iteration statements.

```
 1 /*perfect.c*/
 2 #include <stdio.h>
 3 int main(void)
 4 {
 5      int n;
 6      while(scanf("%d", &n) != EOF) {
 7           int sum = 1;
 8           int divisor;
 9           for(divisor = 2; divisor <= n/2; divisor++)
10                if(n%divisor == 0)
11                     sum += divisor;
12           if(sum == n)
13                printf("%d is perfect\n", n);
14           else
15                printf("%d is not perfect\n", n);
16      }
17 }
```

4.5 Jump Statements

A jump statement causes an unconditional jump to another place. C provides a useful set of jump statements which means that the *goto* statement can be avoided [32]. *Break* and *continue* provide a clean implementation of loop-and-a-half constructions ([24], pp.55-56). In particular, tests take place naturally -- inside the loop body without having to set a flag or force artificial termination conditions.

4.5.1 Break Statement

The *break* statement terminates the smallest enclosing *do*, *for*, *switch*, or *while* statement.

Example 4.8

This function fetches the next line from the standard input into an array of *char*. The *while* statement handles the two extremes (running out of space in the array or encountering end-of-file). *Break* terminates the loop body naturally after dealing with the *NEWLINE* character.

```
 1  /*getline.c*/
 2  #include <stdio.h>
 3  #define NEWLINE    '\n'
 4  int getline(char *s, int max)
 5  {
 6      char c;
 7      char *t = s;
 8      while(--max > 0 && scanf("%c", &c) != EOF) {
 9          *s++ = c;
10          if(c == NEWLINE)
11              break;
12      }
13      *s = '\0';
14      return(s-t);
15  }
```

Some compilers may complain about the implicit cast on line 14.

4.5.2 Continue Statement

The *continue* statement causes control to be passed to the loop-continuation part of the smallest enclosing *do*, *for*, or *while* statement. This is the closing brace at the end of the loop bodies given in Figure 4.1.

```
| do {            | for(...) {      | while(...) {    |
|     ...         |     ...         |     ...         |
|         continue;|         continue;|         continue;|
|     ...         |     ...         |     ...         |
| } while(...);   | }               | }               |
```

Figure 4.1 -- Continuing a Loop

Example 4.9

This program copies the standard input to the standard
output, except that it prints only the first occurrence from
each group of adjacent identical lines. This is a simple
version of the UNIX utility *uniq*. *Getline*() was defined
above in Example 4.8.

```
 1 /*uniq.c*/
 2 #include <stdio.h>
 3 #include <string.h>
 4 #define MAXLINE      200
 5 extern int getline(char *s, int max);
 6 int main(void)
 7 {
 8      char line[MAXLINE];
 9      char prev[MAXLINE];
10      prev[0] = '\0';
11      while(getline(line, MAXLINE) > 0) {
12          if(strcmp(line, prev) == 0)
13              continue;
14          printf("%s", line);
15          strcpy(prev, line);
16      }
17 }
```


The tests against zero (lines 11 and 12) are not
strictly necessary. For example, line 12 could be rewritten
as

```
        if(!strcmp(line, prev))
```

4.5.3 Goto Statement

This is considered harmful [32]. It is an unconditional branch to a labeled statement somewhere in the
current function. Formally, a *goto* statement is never
necessary, and in practice it is easier to write programs
without it.†

Example 4.10

This is the only example containing a *goto* statement.
It is a function that prints the roots of a quadratic equa-
tion. Notice that the program logic is obscure because different cases have been handled by "patching" the code.

```
1  /*quadratic1.c*/
2  #include <math.h>
3  #include <stdio.h>
4  quadratic(double a, double b, double c)
5  {
6       double d = b*b-4*a*c;
7       double r1, r2;
8       if(d == 0)
9            goto EQUAL_ROOTS;
10      if(d > 0) {
11 REAL_ROOTS:    if(a == 0)
12                    goto DEGENERATE_ROOTS;
13           r1 = 0.5*(-b+sqrt(d))/a;
14           r2 = 0.5*(-b-sqrt(d))/a;
15           printf("Real roots\t");
16 PRINT:        printf("%f\t%f\n", r1, r2);
17 DONE:         return;
18      }
19      goto IMAGINARY_ROOTS;
20 DEGENERATE_ROOTS:
21      printf("Degenerate roots\n");
22      goto DONE;
23 IMAGINARY_ROOTS:
24      if(a == 0)
25           goto DEGENERATE_ROOTS;
26      printf("Imaginary roots\n");
27      goto DONE;
28 EQUAL_ROOTS:
29      if(a == 0)
```

†Needless to say *goto* is not used seriously in this
book.

```
30              goto DEGENERATE_ROOTS;
31      r1 = r2 = -0.5*b/a;
32      printf("Equal roots\t");
33      goto PRINT;
34 }
```

4.5.4 Return Statement

The *return* statement causes an immediate exit from the current function. If the *return* statement contains an expression, then the value of that expression is returned to the caller of the function. Some examples are

```
return;          /*no value returned*/
return(-1);      /*return a constant expression*/
return(a+b*c);   /*return the value of an expression*/
return s--;      /*better to write return(s--);*/
```

If there is no expression, no value is returned and, if a value is expected, the behaviour is undefined. Reaching the end of a function body is equivalent to executing a *return* with no expression.

Example 4.11

This function performs a binary search within an ordered array of integers. It returns the position in the array if the key value is present, otherwise it returns -1. Note that array subscripts always start from zero. The *return* statement on line 10 is more elegant than using a *break* statement or setting a flag, both of which would require a test after the *while* statement. It also means that the variable *middle* can be defined local to the inner block (lines 7 to 15).

```
1 /*binary.c*/
2 int binary(int a[], int n, int k)
3 {
4      int low = 0;
5      int high = n;
6      while(low <= high) {
7              int middle = (low+high)/2;
8              if(a[middle] == k)
9                      return(middle);
```

```
10                 if(a[middle] < k)
11                         low = middle+1;
12                 else
13                         high = middle-1;
14         }
15         return(-1);
16 }
```

Assignment 4.1

(a)   Write an equivalent form of the *do* statement   in   terms
      of *if* statements and *while* statements.

(b)   Write an equivalent form of the *while* statement   in
      terms of *if* statements and *do* statements.

(c)   Write an equivalent form of the *switch* statement   in
      terms of *if* statements.

(d)   Write an equivalent form of the *if* statement   in   terms
      of *switch* statements.

Assignment 4.2

      Write a program to print the employee number of the
oldest employee of the NODDY Software Corporation and the
employee number of the longest serving employee. The function call

            scanf("%d/%d/%d", &day, &month, &year)

will read the day, month, and year fields of a date where
they are separated by solidus characters (/). Remember that
the date fields are not at the beginning of a line!

Assignment 4.3

(a)   Rewrite the function for solving quadratic equations
      given in Example 4.10 without using *goto* statements.

(b)   Write a similar function for solving cubic   equations.
      Cardan's   solution   ([33],   pp.118-124) is easy to pro-
      gram.

Chapter 5
Functions and Programs

5.1 Introduction

The effective way to solve a problem is to decompose it into a number of smaller, more manageable problems. This is the only successful way to write a large program -- break it down into small, tractable pieces. Functions do precisely this. They are used to implement a *top-down* method of programming, building on what others have done, and hiding details from those that don't need to know.

C functions are easy and efficient to use. Each program consists of one or more files, each file containing one or more functions. Most well-written C programs consist of many small functions rather than a few large ones. Library functions, such as *scanf()* and *printf()*, are familiar and have been used in previous examples. This chapter is concerned with writing new functions.

The function prototype mechanism is a recent and useful addition to the language. The following sections explain, with examples, how this mechanism co-exists with traditional C.

5.2 Function Declarators

A function declarator consists of a name and a pair of parentheses containing formal parameter information. There are two distinct flavours

(1)   A function prototype. Within the parentheses a parame-
      ter type list declares the types of, and optional iden-
      tifiers for, the formal parameters. If the list ends
      in an ellipsis (...),   there is no information about
      further parameters.† Some examples are

```
int getline(char *s, int n);
int main(int argc, char *argv[]);
int printf(const char *format, ...);
void abort(void);
```

(2)   "Traditional" C.   An optional list of identifiers
      within the parentheses specifying the formal parame-
      ters. The same examples are

```
int getline(s, n);
int main(argc, argv);
int printf();
void abort();
```

    Functions taking a variable number of arguments, like
printf(), can only use the ellipsis notation within a prototype declaration, so the traditional form cannot give <u>any</u>
information about the formal parameters.

5.3 Function Definitions

    A function definition consists of one of the two fla-
vours of function declarator described above, followed by a
compound statement (or block).   There is no semicolon
between the function declarator and the compound statement.

(1)   A minimal function definition is

```
void dummy(void)
{
}
```

    which is a function taking no arguments, doing nothing,
    and not returning a value. To avoid an ambiguity in
    the language, a *typedef* name cannot be used as a formal

---

†The macros in <stdarg.h> (see Section 9.10) are used
to access these arguments.

parameter name.

(2)   Undeclared parameters are taken to be of type *int*, but
       it is better practice to declare all parameters. Simi-
       larly, by default, functions return an *int*. It is good
       practice to include them always as they give a visual
       clue to their use for a human reader.

A function is executed by invoking it. This entails
writing its name followed by an argument list in
parentheses. The formal parameters are initialised to the
values of the *actual parameters* when the function is called.
This mechanism is known as *call by value*. It means that an
actual parameter is never changed by the called function.

Example 5.1

This program, an adaptation of the program in Example
2.2, illustrates a function taking one *int* argument and
returning an *int*. The function, *ctof()*, takes a celsius
temperature as its argument and returns the equivalent
fahrenheit temperature. Each time the function is called
the formal parameter *c* is initialised to the current value
of *celsius*. In all other respects a formal parameter is
treated as an *auto* object effectively declared in the outer-
most block of the function body and having an lvalue.

```
 1 /*ctof2.c*/
 2 #include <stdio.h>
 3 #define LOW     0
 4 #define HIGH    100
 5 #define MULBY   1.8
 6 #define ADDIN   32.5
 7 int ctof(int c)
 8 {
 9      return((int)(c*MULBY+ADDIN));
10 }
11 int main(void)
12 {
13      int celsius;
14      for(celsius = LOW; celsius <= HIGH; celsius++)
15          printf("%3d\t%3d\n", celsius, ctof(celsius));
16 }
```

Example 5.2

This program reverses each line of the standard input and prints the result on the standard output. It illustrates the use of external declarations. External functions are normally compiled separately. Thus the object code versions of *getline*() and *reverse*() must be available during linking of this program (see Section 1.7). *Getline*() was defined in Example 4.8 and *reverse*() is defined in Example 6.2.

```
1 /*reverse2.c*/
2 #include <stdio.h>
3 #define MAXLINE     200
4 extern int getline(char *s, int max);
5 extern void reverse(char *s);
6 int main(void)
7 {
8      char line[MAXLINE];
9      while(getline(line, MAXLINE) > 0) {
10             reverse(line);
11             printf("%s", line);
12     }
13 }
```

The equivalence between a (*char* *) formal parameter and the name of an array will be explained in Section 6.3.

5.4 Function Arguments

A function argument can be any expression other than *void*. Each argument is evaluated, and assigned to the corresponding formal parameter.

(1)   If a function prototype is in scope, the arguments are compared with the formal parameters and converted accordingly. The ellipsis notation (...) in a function prototype causes argument checking and conversion to stop after the last formal parameter declaration. The default argument conversions (see below) are performed on any remaining arguments.

(2)   If no function prototype is in scope, integral promotion is performed (see Section 2.2) and arguments of type *float* are promoted to *double*.

5.5 Command-line Arguments

The function called at program startup is called
main(), and is the only function that may be declared with
either no arguments or two arguments. This special case
reflects the common practice of omitting the arguments to
main() when the program does not reference them.

(1) When function prototypes are used the definition is
written as

```
int main(void)
```

or with two parameters as

```
int main(int argc, char *argv[])
```

where *argc* is the number of command line arguments and
argv is an array of pointers to *char*. The string
pointed to by *argv[0]* is the name by which the program
was invoked, so *argc* is always greater than zero. The
strings pointed to by *argv[1]*, ..., *argv[argc-1]* are
the program arguments. *argv[argc]* is equal to *NULL* to
provide a redundant check for the end of the list.
File names are often passed as arguments to *main()*.

(2) Traditional C programs often contain this definition

```
main(argc, argv)
int argc;
char *argv[];
{
        . . .
}
```

where *main()* returns an *int* by default.

Example 5.3

This program echos its command-line arguments on the
standard output. It is a simple version of the UNIX utility
echo.

```
1 /*echo.c*/
2 #include <stdio.h>
```

```
3 main(int argc, char *argv[])
4 {
5       int i;
6       for(i = 1; i < argc; i++)
7             printf("%s\n", argv[i]);
8 }
```

5.6 Recursion

A function is recursive if it calls itself, either directly or indirectly. In C all functions can be used recursively. Definitions of recursion range from the strong "divide and conquer" [34] to the childhood example given by Rohl ([35], p.1) illustrating an adjectival clause containing another adjectival clause containing ...

```
      This is the cock that crowed in the morn
      That woke the priest all shaven and shorn
      That married the man all tattered and torn
      That kissed the maiden all forlorn
      That milked the cow with the crumpled horn
      That tossed the dog
      That worried the cat
      That killed the rat
      That ate the malt
      That lay in the house that Jack built.

      Figure 5.1 -- The House that Jack Built
```

Example 5.4

Even *main*() can be called recursively. Kelley & Pohl ([13], p.225) give a slightly different version of this recursive program

```
1 /*unendliche.c*/
2 #include <stdio.h>
3 int main(void)
4 {
5       printf("Never ending story\n");
6       main();
7 }
```

Example 5.5

The boringly classic example of recursion computing
values of the factorial function. Once again ([25], p.72)
this example is included for completeness.

```
1 /*factorial.c*/
2 #include <stdio.h>
3 int factorial(int n)
4 {
5       if(n == 0)
6             return(1);
7       return(n*factorial(n-1));
8 }
9 int main(void)
10 {
11      int i;
12      while(scanf("%d", &i) != EOF)
13            printf("%d\t%d\n", i, factorial(i));
14 }
```

Example 5.6

This excellent description of a task ideally suited for
recursive programming was first given by Lawrie Moore ([36],
p.177)

> An attractive myth tells how, in a sacred temple,
> there are three needles of diamonds, on one of
> which originally rested 64 golden disks, all of
> different sizes, forming a conical tower, the nee-
> dle passing through a central hole in each disk.
> The monks of the temple have the task of moving
> all the disks to one of the other two needles, but
> they must observe the sacred laws, which do not
> permit a larger disk ever to rest upon a smaller
> one, and which allow only one disk at a time to be
> moved. When the task is completed, and all 64
> disks have been moved, says the myth, the world
> will come to an end.
> It must be admitted that the satisfaction and
> enjoyment derived by programming the myth does not
> match the thrill of using the pukka diamond nee-
> dles and golden disks in the temple at Hanoi.

Note how *typedef* is used on line 4 to provide a synonym for
an enumeration type (see Section 3.3.1).

```
 1 /*hanoi.c*/
 2 #include <stdio.h>
 3 #define WORLDEND     64
 4 typedef enum {LEFT, MIDDLE, RIGHT} pole;
 5 void printpole(pole p)
 6 {
 7         switch(p) {
 8         case LEFT:
 9                 printf("Left");
10                 break;
11         case MIDDLE:
12                 printf("Middle");
13                 break;
14         case RIGHT:
15                 printf("Right");
16                 break;
17         }
18 }
19 void movedisk(pole source, pole destination)
20 {
21         printpole(source);
22         printf(" to ");
23         printpole(destination);
24         printf("\n");
25 }
26 void move(int n, pole source, pole destination, pole other)
27 {
28         if(n > 1)
29                 move(n-1, source, other, destination);
30         movedisk(source, destination);
31         if(n > 1)
32                 move(n-1, other, destination, source);
33 }
34 int main(void)
35 {
36         int total;
37         scanf("%d", &total);
38         move(total, LEFT, RIGHT, MIDDLE);
39         if(total >= WORLDEND)
40                 printf("World ends now\n");
41 }
```

Assignment 5.1

Write function definitions for the actions described below. Test these functions.

(a) A function taking three arguments of type *int* and returning the largest value.

(b) A function which converts a fahrenheit temperature into a celsius temperature.

(c) A function which computes the highest common factor of its two arguments.

(d) A function for computing Ackerman's function ([35], pp.106-107).

Assignment 5.2

The NODDY Software Corporation transmits telegrams between staff members by grouping a number of telegrams together into a text file and then transmitting the file. The file structure is as follows

• The file consists of a number of variable-length lines of characters.

• Each line contains an integral number of words, separated by space characters. There may be one or more spaces between adjacent words, at the beginning of a line, and at the end of a line.

• A telegram consists of a number of words followed by the special word ZZZZ. The last telegram in the file is the null telegram consisting only of the word ZZZZ. There is no particular relationship between lines and telegrams. A telegram may begin and end anywhere on a line, and may span several lines. Several telegrams may share a line. It can be assumed that the word ZZZZ only appears as described above.

Write a program to analyse the telegrams. For each telegram, a report should show the number of words it contains and the number of words which are oversize (more than twelve characters). The word ZZZZ does not count as a word and the null telegram does not count as an actual telegram. The report should be printed as follows

T	W	V
1	15	2
2	106	0
3	42	4
...		

Assignment 5.3

A sequence such as

0, 1, 1, 2, 3, 5, 8, 13, 21, 34, ...

in which each number is the sum of the preceding two numbers is know as a *Fibonacci* sequence ([37], pp.78-86). The following recursive function could be used to generate numbers in this sequence

```
long fibonacci(long n)
{
        if(n <= 1)
                return(n);
        return(fibonacci(n-2)+fibonacci(n-1));
}
```

(a) Explain why this function is not suitable for computing numbers in the sequence.

(b) Determine how many calls to the function are required in order to calculate *fibonacci(k)*.

(c) If each function invokation takes one micro-second, determine what number in the sequence will take a year to compute.

(d) Write a non-recursive function for computing numbers in the Fibonacci sequence.

Chapter 6
Arrays and Pointers

6.1 Introduction

There is a strong relationship between arrays and
pointers. That is why they are described together in this
chapter. Any array subscripting operation can also be done
with pointers.

6.2 Arrays

An array in C consists of a fixed number of components,
all of the same type. Each component is accessed using an
integral subscript, or index. The indexing of array elements always starts at zero. A one-dimensional array
declaration specifies the <u>size</u> of the array as in

```
        int a[20];        /*a[0], a[1], ..., a[19]*/
```

although it is better programming practice to define the
size of an array as a symbolic constant. This symbolic constant is defined in only one place and it can be used consistently. It is important to remember that the upper bound
of the array is one less than the size. This is a common
mistake to make. Note how the symbolic constant *PRIMES* is
used in the following example.

Example 6.1

This program finds prime numbers using the sieve of
Eratosthenes (3rd Century B.C.). Note the use of *typedef* on
line 5 to declare a boolean type and two symbolic constants.
The cast on line 12 is necessary with traditional C because
sqrt() expects an argument of type *double*. However, if the
header *<math.h>* contains a function prototype for *sqrt()* it
is unnecessary.

```
1  /*sieveprimes.c*/
2  #include <stdio.h>
3  #include <math.h>
4  #define PRIMES 500
5  typedef enum {FALSE, TRUE} boolean;
6  int main(void)
7  {
8       boolean prime[PRIMES];
9       int i, d;
10      for(i = 2; i < PRIMES; i++)
11           prime[i] = TRUE;
12      for(d = 2; d < sqrt((double)PRIMES); d++)
13           if(prime[d])
14                for(i = d; i < PRIMES/d; i++)
15                     prime[i*d] = FALSE;
16      for(i = 2; i < PRIMES; i++)
17           if(prime[i])
18                printf("%d\n", i);
19  }
```

6.2.1 Initialisation

Arrays can be initialised. An example is

        float f[3] = {-1.2, 3.4, 5.6};

If the list of initialisers is shorter than the array size,
the remaining elements are initialised to zero.

If an array is defined without a size and is initial-
ised, its size is implied from the list of initialisers.
The five definitions in Figure 6.1 are equivalent and illus-
trate that a string is only an array of *char*.

```
char Arthur[] = "Dent";

char Arthur[5] = "Dent";

char Arthur[] = {'D', 'e', 'n', 't', '\0'};

char Arthur[5] = {'D', 'e', 'n', 't', '\0'};

char Arthur[5] = {'D', 'e', 'n', 't'};
```

Figure 6.1 -- The Hitch Hiker's Guide to Strings

Why is the sixth possible definition

```
char Arthur[] = {'D', 'e', 'n', 't'};
```

not equivalent to the other five?

6.2.2 Multi-dimensional Arrays

The C language allows arrays of any type, so multi-dimensional arrays are available as arrays of arrays. Figure 6.2 illustrates some array declarations.

```
double vector[3];          /*one dimension*/
char chess[8][8];          /*two dimensions*/
int rubic[6][3][3];        /*three dimensions*/
```

Figure 6.2 -- Array Declarations

Multi-dimensional array definitions can contain initialisers, using either nested lists (fully bracketed initialisation) as in

```
int ackerman[4][5] = {
        {1, 2, 3, 4, 5},
        {2, 3, 4, 5, 6},
        {3, 5, 7, 9, 11},
        {5, 13, 29, 61, 125}};
```

or a single linear list as in the equivalent definition

```
int ackerman[4][5] = {
        1, 2, 3, 4, 5, 2, 3, 4, 5, 6,
        3, 5, 7, 9, 11, 5, 13, 29, 61, 125};
```

When a multi-dimensional array is used as a formal parameter of a function, the sizes of all but the last dimension must be given explicitly. Consider the following function definition

```
void clear(char board[8][8]);
{
        ...
}
```

for clearing a chess board. The last dimension is not required, but is included for clarity.

6.3 Pointers

Pointers and arrays are used in very similar ways to access objects. However, the differences between them are subtle and important.

(1) An array name is a constant pointer (constant address). When an array is defined, the compiler allocates a base address and sufficient storage for the elements of the array. An array name is never an lvalue.

(2) A pointer is an object that contains the address of another object. It is always an lvalue. Pointer arithmetic is very powerful. If p is a pointer to an object, then the expression $p+1$ is a pointer to the next object of the same type. Thus pointer expressions such as $p++$, $p+i$, and $p -= j$ are all valid. If p and q are both pointers to the same type of object, then the expression $p-q$ yields a signed integer† that is the number of such objects between p and q.

The following two examples demonstrate this equivalence between arrays and pointers.

---

†Of type $ptrdiff\_t$ from <stddef.h> (see Section 9.11).

Example 6.2

This function reverses its character string argument. The end of string marker, '\0', is not made the first character. While swapping characters, i is incremented towards the end of the string and j is decremented towards the beginning of the string. Reverse() is rewritten using pointers in Example 6.3. Strlen() returns the length of its string argument, excluding the NUL terminator (see Section 9.14.5).

```
1 /*reverse1.c*/
2 #include <string.h>
3 void reverse(char s[])
4 {
5      int i;
6      int j = strlen(s)-1;
7      for(i = 0; i < j; i++) {
8           char temp = s[i];
9           s[i] = s[j];
10          s[j] = temp;
11          j--;
12     }
13 }
```

The compiler always translates "array of ..." into "pointer to ..." for its formal parameters. It is this equivalence that makes the previous Example 6.2 work.

Example 6.3

This function reverses the character string passed to it as an argument. It is the pointer version of Example 6.2. The character array s is replaced by a pointer to a character, *s. Thus *s is used equivalently to s[i] and *t is used equivalently to s[j].

```
1 /*reverse3.c*/
2 #include <string.h>
3 void reverse(char *s)
4 {
5      char *t = s+strlen(s)-1;
6      while(s < t) {
7           char temp = *s;
8           *s++ = *t;
9           *t-- = temp;
10     }
```

```
11 }
```

The use of *void* * (pointer to void) as a generic
pointer type is taken from C++, a dialect of C developed at
AT&T Bell Laboratories [38]. Consult the memory management
functions (see Section 9.13.3) for examples.

Assignment 6.1

The following function is meant to generate finite seg-
ments of the Hilbert Matrix ([39], p.33) given by

$$
\begin{array}{llll}
1 & 1/2 & 1/3 & \ldots \\
1/2 & 1/3 & 1/4 & \ldots \\
1/3 & 1/4 & 1/5 & \ldots \\
\ldots
\end{array}
$$

```
1 /*hilbert.c*/
2 void hilbert(double a[], int n)
3 {
4       int i, j;
5       for(i = 1; i <= n; i++)
6            for(j = 1; j <= n; j++)
7                 a[i, j] = 1.0/(i+j-1);
8 }
```

(a)   Explain why the function doesn't produce the required
      result.

(b)   Describe what the function does generate.

(c)   Rewrite the function to generate the correct matrix.

Assignment 6.2

Write a program to print a histogram showing the salary
distribution of the employees at the NODDY Software Corporation. Partition the salaries into the ten ranges ((£0 ..
£3,000], (£3,000 .. £6,000], ..., (£27,000 .. £30,000]. The
histogram should be printed as follows

```
8 |             * *                              |
7 |             * *                              |
6 |        * *  * *                              |
5 |        * *  * *  * *                          |
4 |        * *  * *  * *                          |
3 |        * *  * *  * *                          |
2 |   * *  * *  * *  * *  * *                      |
1 |   * *  * *  * *  * *  * *  * *       * *      |
--+----------------------------------------+
   | 3   6   9  12  15  18  21  24  27  30 |
```

Assignment 6.3

There are many applications where it would be convenient to declare arrays with a *lower bound* other than
zero. Consider putting such a proposal to a C language
standards committee. Some points to bear in mind are given
below.

• What form does the declaration take?

• Is there a default lower bound?

• Can both forms of the declaration co-exist?

• What ramifications will there be when considering the
equivalence of arrays and pointers?

• What precedents are there for such a change?

Chapter 7
Structures and Unions

7.1 Introduction

A structure is an ordered sequence of many named objects, possibly of different types, grouped together as a single object.† A union is an overlapping sequence of named members. Structures and unions have the same form. In addition, a member of a structure or union may be declared to consist of a specified number of bits. These *bit-fields* are covered in Section 7.4.

7.2 Structures

Structures group together related information, as in

```
        struct {
                char name[40];
                int rating;
                float price;
        } le_gavroche;
```

A member of the structure is referenced using dot notation as in

---

†Structures are often called *records* in other languages.

```
    strcpy(le_gavroche.name, "Le Gavroche");
    le_gavroche.rating = 17;
    le_gavroche.price = 46.00;
```

The above definition uses an *explicit* structure. It is usually better to declare the structure in such a way that a name is associated with the type as in

```
        struct restaurant {
                char name[40];
                int rating;
                float price;
        };
```

The so called structure tag, *restaurant*, can now be used in declarations and definitions as in

```
    struct restaurant tante_clair, gay_hussar;
```

Alternatively, a *typedef* declaration (see Section 3.7) can be used

```
        typedef struct {
                char name[40];
                int rating;
                float price;
        } restaurant;
```

with declarations and definitions taking the form

```
    restaurant langans[2], *chez_nico;
```

The method of accessing members of structures remains the same, namely dot notation.

```
    strcpy(langans[0].name, "Langan's Brasserie");
    strcpy(langans[1].name, "Langan's Bistro");
    tante_clair.rating = 16;
    gay_hussar.price = 20.0;
```

In common with other types, structures can be assigned, initialised, passed as parameters to functions, and returned by functions. Unfortunately structures cannot be compared for equality, due to the problem of holes in structures (see Section 7.4).

Example 7.1

A simple date consists of three parts, namely values representing the day, month, and year. Here is a type declaration and two definitions. Note that structures can be initialised, as can all aggregates.

```
1 /*date1.h*/
2 struct date {
3      short day;
4      short month;
5      short year;
6 } my_birthday = {10, 11, 1945},
7   *your_birthday = NULL;
```

Because C frequently uses pointers to structures there is an operator, ->, for selecting a member of a structure from the pointer. This saves having to use parentheses around a dereference operation.

```
your_birthday->month    /*same as (*your_birthday).month*/
```

Example 7.2

Structure declarations can be nested. Here is the structure declaration for employees of the NODDY Software Corporation.

```
1 /*person.h*/
2 #define MAXNAME 20
3 struct person {
4      int number;
5      char name[MAXNAME+1];
6      int salary;
7      int manager;
8      struct date birthday;
9      struct date startdate;
10 };
```

Example 7.3

Structure declarations can be self-referential. This reference has to be in the form of a pointer† otherwise the declaration expands indefinitely (and is invalid). Consider this example of a singly-linked list

```
        +----+----+   +----+----+           +----+----+
    ─>|Item|Next| ─>|Item|Next| ─>... ─>|Item|Next|
        +----+----+   +----+----+           +----+----+
```

where each *node* is declared as follows

```
1 /*slink.h*/
2 struct node {
3       struct person item;
4       struct node *next;
5 };
```

In common with other block structured languages permitting forward references there is a problem with structure (and union) tags. The declaration of two mutually referencing structures as

```
struct a {struct b *pb; ...};
struct b {struct a *pa; ...};
```

will not work if *struct b* is already declared in an enclosing block. The first field of *struct a* refers to the older declaration. A special construct is used to hide an outer declaration

```
struct b;
struct a {struct b *pb; ...};
struct b {struct a *pa; ...};
```

7.3 Unions

A *union* is an object that may, at a given time, contain any one of several named members. It can be thought of as a

---

†Or a nest of objects containing at least one pointer.

structure whose members overlap and whose size is sufficient to hold the largest member as in

```
union flint {
        float f;
        int i;
} lock;
```

At most one of the members can be stored in a union at any time.   The notation used to access a member of a union is the same as that to access a member of a structure as in

```
lock.f = 1.23;
```

Unions are used to conserve storage by overlaying the storage for the different members.   See Example 7.4 and Example 7.5 for some interesting uses.

7.4 Bit-Fields

It is possible to "pack" several objects into one structure containing several flavours of *int*. Where possible a bit-field that follows another bit-field is packed into the same *int*. It is implementation-dependent whether a bit-field can straddle an *int* boundary.† Such fields are put into the next *int*.   The following example illustrates a desperate attempt to save space on storage for objects of type *date*.

```
1 /*date2.h*/
2 struct date {
3        unsigned short day : 5;
4        unsigned short month : 4;
5        unsigned year : 11;
6 };
```

A bit-field declaration with no declarator, but only a colon and width, indicates an unnamed field used for padding to conform to externally-imposed layouts, e.g. machine word boundaries.

---

†A field forced to start on a new boundary will leave a *hole*.

Example 7.4

This example of a *union* and bit-fields illustrates a technique for accessing a 16-bit machine word in different formats.

```
 1  /*words.h*/
 2  struct wbits {
 3        unsigned bit0   : 1;
 4        unsigned bit1   : 1;
 5        unsigned bit2   : 1;
 6        unsigned bit3   : 1;
 7        unsigned bit4   : 1;
 8        unsigned bit5   : 1;
 9        unsigned bit6   : 1;
10        unsigned bit7   : 1;
11        unsigned bit8   : 1;
12        unsigned bit9   : 1;
13        unsigned bit10  : 1;
14        unsigned bit11  : 1;
15        unsigned bit12  : 1;
16        unsigned bit13  : 1;
17        unsigned bit14  : 1;
18        unsigned bit15  : 1;
19  };
20  struct wbytes {
21        unsigned byte0  : 8;
22        unsigned byte1  : 8;
23  };
24  union word {
25        unsigned whole : 16;
26        struct wbytes byte;
27        struct wbits bit;
28  };
```

Example 7.5

The following example illustrates the use of *struct*, *union*, and bit-fields, together with *typedef*. These declarations outline the structure of Initialisation and Termination Commands within FTP as presented in the "Blue Book" ([29], p.166).

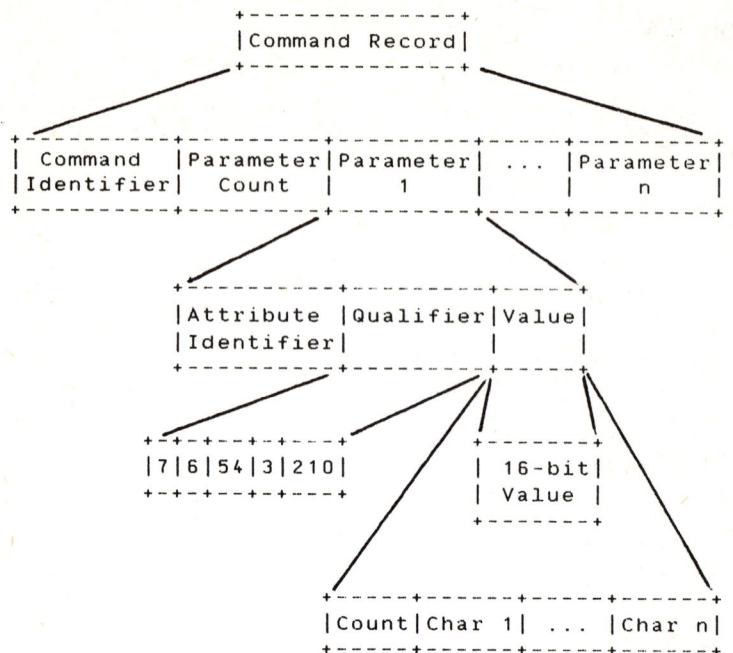

Figure 7.1 -- FTP Command Structure

This is a header file containing all the declarations.
Note that two one-bit fields (lines 7 and 9) are currently
unallocated.

```
 1  /*ftp.h*/
 2  #define MAXPARAMS    255
 3  #define MAXCHARS     255
 4  typedef unsigned char octet;
 5  typedef struct {
 6      unsigned operator : 3;
 7      unsigned : 1;
 8      unsigned format : 2;
 9      unsigned : 1;
10      unsigned monitor : 1;
11  } qualifier;
12  typedef struct {
13      octet count;
14      char c[MAXCHARS];
15  } string;
16  typedef union {
17      short n;
```

```
18        string s;
19 } value;
20 typedef struct {
21        octet identifier;
22        qualifier q;
23        value v;
24 } param;
25 typedef struct {
26        octet identifier;
27        octet count;
28        param p[MAXPARAMS];
29 } command;
```

Assignment 7.1

In 1891 a mountaineer by the name of Sir Hugh T. Munro, Bart. of Lindertis carried out a survey of the mountains in Scotland over 3,000 ft. There were 283 mountains in this original list, and they collectively became known as Munros. The nine mountains over 4,000 ft are given in Figure 7.2.

Height	Name	Grid Reference
4409	Ben Nevis	NN.1671
4296	Ben Macdui	NN.9898
4250	Braeriach	NN.9599
4236	Cairn Toul	NN.9697
4127	Sgor an Lochain Uaine	NN.9597
4085	Cairngorm	NJ.0004
4054	Aonach Beag	NN.1971
4012	Carn Mor Dearg	NN.1772
4002	Aonach Mor	NN.1973

Figure 7.2 -- Munros over 4,000 ft.

Declare types for the Munros as

(a)   Three arrays.

(b)   An array of structures, each structure containing three members.

(c)   A structure of three arrays.

Assignment 7.2

The chair of NODDY Software Corporation is J.D. Bullock who imposes a strict management hierarchy (see Section 1.8). The following structure can hold employee details according to this management hierarchy

```
1 /*mtree.h*/
2 struct node {
3        struct person *info;
4        struct node *across;
5        struct node *down;
6 };
```

where the *info* field points to an employee's record, where the *across* field links employees managed by the same person, and the *down* field points to an employee being managed.

(a) Write a program that inputs the employee information from the standard input and constructs the management tree. Use Example 7.2.

(b) Using this tree, compute the name of the person who manages the most people and the salary of the "lowliest" employee.

Assignment 7.3

(a) Extend the structure declaration for a restaurant given in Section 7.2 to include other importants details such as address, telephone number, opening times, cuisine, etc. As an example look at the entry for *Fawlty Towers* in the Good Food Guide ([40], pp.22-24).

(b) Complete a suitable software package for manipulating such information about restaurants.

(c) Sell your package to one (or more) of the numerous Guides.

Chapter 8
The Preprocessor

8.1 Introduction

The preprocessor is used to extend the power and notation of the compiler. Lines that begin with a # in the
first column are called *control lines*, and these communicate
with the preprocessor. It is important to remember that the
preprocessor does not know any C!

8.2 Source File Inclusion

A control line of the form

        #include "filename"

causes the preprocessor to replace the line with a copy of
the specified file. The quotes are mandatory. A search for
the file starts in the current directory† and then in standard places (usually */usr/include*). A control line of the
form

        #include <filename>

causes the preprocessor to look for the file only in the
standard places. Nested include files are allowed. In this
case there is no explicit search rule, but most

---

†This is implementation-dependent, though well defined
on UNIX systems.

implementations search relative to the same *current direc-tory*.

8.3 Macro Replacement

Macro processing is an interesting topic in its own right [41] with a wide range of *special-purpose* and *general-purpose* tools available. This preprocessor sits roughly in the middle. It is (mostly) ignorant of the C language and manipulates tokens within a line-oriented grammar.

The definition of a macro (simple or with arguments) is turned off for the duration of the expansion of that macro. This avoids the possible problem of a preprocessor which encounters the macro name in its expansion suffering "recursive death".

8.3.1 Simple Macros

A control line of the form

```
#define identifier token-sequence
```

defines a *macro* such that subsequent occurrences of the identifier (the macro name) are replaced by the specified sequence of tokens. The replacement string is rescanned for further macros. Here are some examples.

```
#define EOF      (-1)
#define MAXSIZE  250
#define NEWLINE  '\n'
#define PI       3.14159265
#define TWOPI    (2*PI)
#define YEAR     (&my_birthday.year)
```

This facility is used to define manifest constants or "shorthand" names which, conventionally, are written in upper-case to identify them to human readers. Macro replacement is based on tokens which means that sequences such as *MAX SIZE* and *NEWLINES* will not be expanded.

8.3.2 Macros with Arguments

A control line of the form

#define identifier(identifier-list) token-sequence

defines a macro with (optional) arguments. Note that there
is no white space between the macro name and the following
left parenthesis. Here are some examples.

```
#define HALF(x) x/2
#define SQR(x) (x)*(x)
#define TWICE(x) (2*(x))
```

It is important to use parentheses within macro definitions because the expansions take place during a (possibly
notional) pre-pass. Thus only the last of the three examples above is safe within any context, as the expansions in
Figure 8.1 show.

```
HALF(a+b)           a+b/2
a/SQR(b)            a/(b)*(b)
a/TWICE(b+c)        a/(2*(b+c))
```

Figure 8.1 -- Whoops, Wrong Again Department

Example 8.1

This function reverses the character string passed to
it as an argument. It illustrates a popular use for macros
and the bitwise exclusive-OR operator. Compare it with
Example 6.3.

```
1  /*reverse4.c*/
2  #include <string.h>
3  #define SWAP(x, y) {x ^= y; y ^= x; x ^= y;}
4  reverse(char *s)
5  {
6      char *t = s+strlen(s)-1;
7      for(; s < t; s++, t--)
8          SWAP(*s, *t)
9  }
```

It is important to bear in mind that the function *reverse()* is no shorter than the function in Example 6.3. However, the loop has to be different. If lines 7 and 8 above were replaced by

```
while(s < t)
        SWAP(*s++, *t--)
```

the function would not work. Why?

8.3.3 String-ising

The # operator may only be used inside a #*define* expansion. It causes the following formal parameter name to be replaced by a string constant (literal) constructed from the actual parameter. Given the following macro definition

```
#define DEBUG(s) printf(#s " = %d", s);
```

the macro call *DEBUG(kevin)* results in, after concatenation of string literals (see Section 1.4.4), the following

```
printf("kevin = %d", kevin);
```


8.3.4 Concatenation

The ## operator within a macro expansion concatenates the two tokens on either side of it into a new token. This created token is available for further macro replacement. Given the following macro definition

```
#define PRINT(s, t) printf(#s #t " = %d", s##t);
```

the macro call *PRINT(x, 2)* results in, after string-ising and concatenation, the following

```
printf("x2 = %d", x2);
```

8.4 Undef

A control line of the form

#undef identifier

causes the macro definition (if there is one) to be forgot-
ten.

8.5 Conditional Inclusion

A control line of the form

#if constant-expression

causes the preprocessor to evaluate the expression in order
to determine whether the subsequent section is to be compiled (non-zero) or not (zero). This section is terminated
by a control line of the form

#endif

The controlling constant expression must evaluate to type
int and not contain a *sizeof* operator, a cast, or an
enumeration constant. It may contain unary expressions of
the forms

defined identifier
defined(identifier)

which evaluate to one if the identifier is currently defined
as a macro name.† Additional control lines of the form

#elif constant-expression

or

#else

---

†This means that *defined* is an operator and therefore
cannot be defined as a macro by a perverse user!

can be used to form nested inclusion sections. Consider this example

```
#if HUGE_MACHINE
    ...
#elif LARGE_MACHINE
    ...
#elif SMALL_MACHINE
    ...
#elif TINY_MACHINE
    ...
#else
    ...
#endif
```

which neatly specifies one of three sections to be compiled.

Excluded source code is scanned for additional control lines which are verified for syntactic correctness. However, #*include* files are not read.

It is still possible to use the older, additional, forms

```
#ifdef identifier
#ifndef identifier
```

to test whether an identifier has been defined or not, but this is not as general as using the operator *defined* in a boolean expression.

8.6 Line Control

A control line of the form

```
#line integer filename
```

causes the compiler to behave as if the line number of the next source line, __*LINE*__, is specified by the (decimal) integer. If present, the current input file name, __*FILE*__, is changed to *filename*. This feature is used by other compilers generating C programs.

8.7 Error

This preprocessing directive causes the compiler to terminate and produce a diagnostic message (the remainder of the line). For example, the control line

#error Real programmers don't eat Quiche.

would only be used in real emergencies, like April Fool's day.

8.8 Pragma

This directive provides a universal method for passing information to the compiler. The result is implementation-dependent! For example, this contrl line

#pragma Do not pass Go, do not collect £200

would only make sense to the Monopolies Commission.

8.9 Null Directive

Control lines containing only # can be used for spacing and layout. They are ignored.

8.10 Predefined Macros

The macros described in Figure 8.2 are the only macros that are predefined within the preprocessor. They cannot be redefined or undefined; this is a recognition that they have special built-in properties.

__DATE__	The date of translation in the form "Mmm dd yyyy".
__FILE__	The presumed name of the source file.
__LINE__	The current source line number.
__STDC__	The value 1. It indicates whether the compiler conforms to the standard or not. Future versions of the standard could define it as 2, 3, ...
__TIME__	The time of translation in the form "hh:mm:ss".

Figure 8.2 -- Predefined Macros in the Preprocessor

Assignment 8.1

Consider the following macro definitions. All of them do not work as intended. Write correct versions.

(a)   `#define PI 4*atan(1.0)`

(b)   `#define INT (x) (int)(x)`

(c)   `#define FALSE(x) ((x) = 0)`

(d)   `#define SHOW(x) printf("x = %d", x);`

(e)   `#define FACT(n) (n ? n*FACT(n-1) : 1)`

Assignment 8.2

Define a set of macros that extract fields and other attributes from the employee records of the NODDY Software Corporation. Two examples could be

```
#define SALARY(x) x.salary
#define NAMELEN(x) strlen(x.name)
```

Another possibility is a macro that takes a *struct date* and returns the corresponding Julian (ordinal) date in the form *yyyyddd*. This simplifies the comparison of dates.

Assignment 8.3

Most operating systems provide a macro processor and it may be more convenient to use one of these rather than the C preprocessor which is fairly limited. Investigate other macro processors. Some suitable general-purpose macro processors are GPM [42], ML/1 [43], and M4 [44]. The latter is available on UNIX.

94

Chapter 9
Library Functions

9.1 Introduction

Every library function or object is associated with a
header file. The preprocessor directive #*include* is used to
make the contents of the header file available (see Section
8.2). Headers may be included in any order, and more than
once. A header should be included before any reference to
an object defined in that header.

There are a couple of restrictions involving names
relating to libraries and headers.

(1) All external identifiers defined by a library (and
therefore appearing in a header) are reserved. Thus no
user supplied external name may match a library name,
even if it has the same specification.

(2) All identifiers beginning with an underscore are
reserved for use in libraries.

9.2 <assert.h> – Diagnostics

This header declares one function and refers to one
macro

                              NDEBUG

which is <u>not</u> defined by <assert.h>. If *NDEBUG* is defined
when <assert.h> is included, then *assert()* has no effect,
and is defined to be the null statement.

The macro

          void assert(int expression);

puts diagnostics into programs. If *expression* is false
(zero) then information about the assertion is written on
the standard error file followed by a call to *abort()* (see
Section 9.13.4). If *expression* is true (non-zero) no value
is returned.

9.3 <ctype.h> – Character Handling

     This header declares several functions for testing
characters and mapping characters. The underlying character
set is implementation-dependent, but in ASCII the printing
characters are from 040 (space) to 0176 (tilde), and the
control characters are from 0 (NUL) to 037 (us) plus 0177
(del).† The ASCII character set is given in Appendix B.

     The behaviour of these functions is affected by the
current locale. See Section 9.6 for more details.

9.3.1 Character Testing Functions

     These testing functions return a non-zero value (true)
if and only if the argument conforms to the description of
the function.

*   int isalnum(int c);
     Test for any letter or digit.

*   int isalpha(int c);
     Test for any letter.

*   int iscntrl(int c);
     Test for any control character.

*   int isdigit(int c);
     Test for any decimal digit.

---

†Remember that integral constants with a leading zero
are in octal.

- `int isgraph(int c);`
  Test for any printing character except space.

- `int islower(int c);`
  Test for any lower-case letter.

- `int isprint(int c);`
  Test for any printing character including space.

- `int ispunct(int c);`
  Test for any punctuation character except space, a digit, or a letter.

- `int isspace(int c);`
  Test for the white-space characters (space, form feed, newline, carriage return, horizontal tab, or vertical tab).

- `int isupper(int c);`
  Test for any upper-case letter.

- `int isxdigit(int c);`
  Test for any hexadecimal digit.

9.3.2 Character Case Mapping Functions

These two functions provide implementation-independent mapping between upper- and lower-case characters.

- `int tolower(int c);`
  If the argument is an upper-case letter return the corresponding lower-case letter, otherwise return the argument unchanged.

- `int toupper(int c);`
  If the argument is a lower-case letter return the corresponding upper-case letter, otherwise return the argument unchanged.

Names beginning with *is* and *to*, when followed by lower-case letters, are subject to future use within `<ctype.h>`.

9.4 `<float.h>` – Characteristics of Floating Types

This header defines several macros that expand to

expressions† defining implementation-dependent limits and parameters. These quantities are useful for numerical analysis. The values given in Figure 9.1 are the minimum magnitudes that are allowed for a particular implementation ([2], pp.14-16).

---

†Only *FLT_RADIX* must be a constant expression.

DBL_DIG	6
DBL_EPSILON	1E-5
DBL_EXP_DIG	
DBL_MANT_DIG	
DBL_MAX	1E+37
DBL_MAX_10_EXP	(+37)
DBL_MAX_EXP	
DBL_MIN	1E-37
DBL_MIN_10_EXP	(-37)
DBL_MIN_EXP	
DBL_NEG_EPS	1E-5
DBL_NEG_EPS_EXP	
DBL_POS_EPS	1E-5
DBL_POS_EPS_EXP	
FLT_DIG	6
FLT_EPSILON	1E-5
FLT_EXP_DIG	
FLT_GUARD	0
FLT_MANT_DIG	
FLT_MAX	1E+37
FLT_MAX_10_EXP	(+37)
FLT_MAX_EXP	
FLT_MIN	1E-37
FLT_MIN_10_EXP	(-37)
FLT_MIN_EXP	
FLT_NEG_EPS	1E-5
FLT_NEG_EPS_EXP	
FLT_NORMALISE	0
FLT_POS_EPS	1E-5
FLT_POS_EPS_EXP	
FLT_RADIX	2
FLT_ROUNDS	0
LDBL_DIG	6
LDBL_EPSILON	1E-5
LDBL_EXP_DIG	
LDBL_MANT_DIG	
LDBL_MAX	1E+37
LDBL_MAX_10_EXP	(+37)
LDBL_MAX_EXP	
LDBL_MIN	1E-37
LDBL_MIN_10_EXP	(-37)
LDBL_MIN_EXP	
LDBL_NEG_EPS	1E-5
LDBL_NEG_EPS_EXP	
LDBL_POS_EPS	1E-5
LDBL_POS_EPS_EXP	

Figure 9.1 -- Macros in <float.h>

In Figure 9.1, a missing value indicates that there is no minimum specified.

9.5 <limits.h> – Sizes of Integral Types

This header defines several macros that expand into implementation-dependent constant expressions. The values given in Figure 9.2 are the minimum magnitudes that are allowed for a particular implementation ([2], pp.13-14).

```
|  CHAR_BIT  |  8                 |
|  CHAR_MAX  |  See below.        |
|  CHAR_MIN  |  See below.        |
|  INT_MAX   |  (+32767)          |
|  INT_MIN   |  (-32767)          |
|  LONG MAX  |  (+2147483647)     |
|  LONG_MIN  |  (-2147483647)     |
|  SCHAR_MAX |  (+127)            |
|  SCHAR_MIN |  (-127)            |
|  SHRT_MAX  |  (+32767)          |
|  SHRT_MIN  |  (-32767)          |
|  UCHAR_MAX |  255U              |
|  UINT_MAX  |  65535U            |
|  ULONG_MAX |  4294967295U       |
|  USHRT_MAX |  65535U            |
```

Figure 9.2 -- Macros in <limits.h>

If the value of an object of type *char* sign-extends when used in an expression then

```
CHAR_MIN = SCHAR_MIN
CHAR_MAX = SCHAR_MAX
```

otherwise, if the value does not sign extend then

```
CHAR_MIN = 0
CHAR_MAX = UCHAR_MAX
```

9.6 <locale.h> – Localisation

This header defines several macros and declares one function. The macros, which expand to integer constant expressions, are given in Figure 9.3. They are suitable for use as the first argument to *setlocale()*.

LC_ALL	The entire locale.
LC_COLLATE	Affects the behaviour of strcoll().
LC_CTYPE	Affects the behaviour of the functions in <ctype.h>.
LC_NUMERIC	Affects the decimal-point character in various functions.
LC_TIME	Affects the behaviour of strftime().

Figure 9.3 -- Macros in <locale.h>

- char *setlocale(int category, const char *locale);
  Interrogate or change parts of the program's locale.
  If locale is NULL the function returns a string associated with the specified category. Otherwise, locale is one of a number of implementation-dependent strings. The string "C" specifies the minimal environment for C translation and "" specifies the native environment. The function returns NULL if either category or locale are invalid. See also strftime() (Section 9.15).

9.7 <math.h> – Mathematics

This header defines three macros and declares several mathematical functions. For historic reasons it is only defined for double quantities. The existing names, suffixed with f or l are reserved for the definition of float and long double libraries.

For all functions a domain error occurs if an input argument is outside the domain for which the function is defined. In this case errno takes the value of EDOM. Similarly a range error occurs if a result of the function cannot be represented as a double. In this case errno takes the value of ERANGE and the function returns HUGE_VAL. Errno is defined in <stddef.h> (see Section 9.11).

EDOM	A *domain error* occurs if an input argument is outside the domain over which the function is defined.
ERANGE	A *range error* occurs if the result of the function cannot be represented as a *double* value.
HUGE_VAL	If the magnitude of the result is so large the function returns this value with the same sign as the correct value of the function.

Figure 9.4 -- Macros in <math.h>

9.7.1 Trigonometric Functions

These functions work in radians rather than degrees.

- double acos(double x);
  Return the arc cosine of x in the range [0, π].

- double asin(double x);
  Return the arc sine of x in the range [-π/2, π/2].

- double atan(double x);
  Return the arc tangent of x in the range (-π/2, π/2).

- double atan2(double y, double x);
  Return the arc tangent of y/x in the range (-π, π] using the signs of both arguments to determine the correct quadrant. A domain error occurs if both arguments are zero.

- double cos(double x);
  Return the cosine of x.

- double sin(double x);
  Return the sine of *x*.

- double tan(double x);
  Return the tangent of *x*.

The range of *atan()* is defined as an open interval in accordance with mathematical practice.

9.7.2 Hyperbolic Functions

These functions work in radians rather than degrees. Range errors can occur.

- double cosh(double x);
  Return the hyperbolic cosine of *x*.

- double sinh(double x);
  Return the hyperbolic sine of *x*.

- double tanh(double x);
  Return the hyperbolic tangent of *x*.

9.7.3 Exponential and Logarithmic Functions

The functions *frexp()*, *ldexp()*, and *modf()* are primitives used by the remainder of the library. Range errors can occur, for compatibility with IEEE P854.

- double exp(double x);
  Return the exponential function of *x*.

- double frexp(double value, int *exp);
  Decompose a floating-point number into a normalised fraction and an integral power of two. The function returns a value *x* with magnitude in the interval [, 1) such that *value* equals *x* times two raised to the power *exp. If value* is zero, both parts of the result are zero.

- double ldexp(double x, int exp);
  Return the value of *x* times 2 raised to the power *exp*.

- double log(double x);
  Return the natural logarithm of *x*. A range error occurs if the argument is zero.

- `double log10(double x);`
  Return the base-ten logarithm of x. A range error occurs if the argument is zero.

- `double modf(double value, double *iptr);`
  Return the signed fractional part of *value* and store the signed integral part in *iptr*.

9.7.4 Power Functions

- `double pow(double x, double y);`
  Return the value of x raised to the power y.

- `double sqrt(double x);`
  Return the non-negative square root of x. A domain error occurs if the argument is negative.

9.7.5 Integer and Absolute Value Functions

There is no absolute value operator in the language. It is felt that a built-in function can provide an efficient implementation.

- `double ceil(double x);`
  Return the smallest integer not less than x, expressed as a *double*.

- `double fabs(double x);`
  Return the absolute value of x.

- `double floor(double x);`
  Return the largest integer not greater than x, expressed as a *double*.

- `double fmod(double x, double y);`
  Return the floating-point remainder of x/y, or x if y is zero.

9.8 <setjmp.h> – Non-local Jumps

This header declares one type and two functions for bypassing the normal function call and return mechanisms.

The type is

jmp_buf

which is an array type suitable for holding environment
information.

• void longjmp(jmp_buf env, int val);
  Restore the environment saved by the most recent call
  to *setjmp()*. A call to *longjmp()* results in the program continuing from a call to *setjmp()* returning the
  value given by *val*. If *val* is zero, *setjmp()* returns
  the value one.

• int setjmp(jmp_buf env);
  Save the calling environment in *env* for later use by
  longjmp(). After a direct call, *setjmp()* returns the
  value zero. If the return is from a call to *longjmp()*
  the returned value is non-zero. This function can only
  be called from within simple expressions, i.e. those
  that don't need temporary storage.

9.9 <signal.h> – Signal Handling

This header defines several macros and declares one
type and two functions. The type is

sig_atomic_t

which is the integral type of an object that can be modified
as an atomic entry in the presence of asynchronous interrupts.

Several of the macro names, *SIGFPE*, etc., have their
roots in PDP-11 [45] hardware technology, but the names are
too entrenched to change. An implementation is not required
to deal with <u>any</u> hardware interrupts if it so chooses.

SIG_IGN	Used as an argument to *signal()* to indicate that a given signal is to be ignored.
SIG_DFL	Used as an argument to *signal()* to indicate that a given signal is to be handled in a default (but implementation-dependent) manner.
SIG_ERR	Returned by *signal()* to indicate an erroneous call.
SIGABRT	Used to indicate abnormal termination.
SIGFPE	Floating-point exception. Usually zero divide or overflow.
SIGILL	Illegal instruction.
SIGINT	Interrupt. Usually *del* or *break* from the keyboard.
SIGSEGV	Segmentation violation. Usually an invalid access to an object.
SIGTERM	Termination request. This allows a process to terminate gracefully

Figure 9.5 -- Signals in <signal.h>

- `void (*signal(int sig, void (*func)(int)))(int);`
A call to *signal()* specifies what action to take when a particular signal is raised. There are three possibilities.

(1) If *func* is *SIG_DFL* default handling for that signal will occur.

(2) If *func* is *SIG_IGN* the signal will be ignored.

(3) Otherwise, *func* points to a function that is called when the signal is raised. The equivalent of

`(*func)(sig);`

is executed. The result of executing a *return* statement within this function is implementation-dependent and extremely dodgy.

Signal() returns the previous value of *func* associated

with the signal *sig*.

- int raise(int sig);
  Send the signal *sig* to the executing program. It returns zero if successful.

    Names beginning with *SIG* are reserved for implementations to add their local names to <signal.h>. This means that users should not use such names in programs which include <signal.h>.

9.10 <stdarg.h> – Variable Arguments

    This header declares one type and one function, and defines two macros for advancing through the argument list of a function. The type is

                              va_list

which is an array type suitable for holding the information needed by the macro *va_arg()* and the function *va_end()*.

void va_start(va_list ap, *argN*);	This macro initialises *ap* for subsequent use by *va_arg()* and *va_end()*. The parameter *argN* is the formal parameter immediately preceding the ellipses.
type va_arg(va_list ap, *type*);	This macro expands to an expression that has the type and value of the next argument in the call. The first call after a call to *va_start* returns the value of the argument after *argN*.

Figure 9.6 -- Macros in <stdarg.h>

- void va_end(va_list ap);
  Clean up the variable argument list *ap*. It must be called from within the body of the function having the variable arguments.

9.11 <stddef.h> – Standard Definitions

This header defines two types and three macros.

ptrdiff_t	The signed integral type of the result of subtracting two pointers.
size_t	The unsigned integral type of the result of the *sizeof* operator.

Figure 9.7 -- Types in <stddef.h>

Including any header that references one of these types or macros will also define it. This is an exception to the usual library rule that each macro or function belongs to exactly one header.

NULL	Implementation-dependent null pointer constant.
offsetof(*type*, *identifier*)	The offset in bytes from the beginning of a structure designated by *type*, of the member *identifier*.
errno	A modifiable lvalue which is set to a positive error code by several library functions. It is of type *volatile int*.

Figure 9.8 -- Macros in <stddef.h>

9.12 <stdio.h> – Input/Output

This header declares two types, several macros, and a number of functions for performing input and output. These functions use a *file pointer* for referencing I/O streams. The unbuffered services use a *file descriptor* (a small integer) for referencing streams (see Appendix C). The types are

FILE

which is a structure holding information about an open file, and

fpos_t

which is an object type capable of storing the information needed to specify uniquely every position within a file. The macros are given in Figure 9.9.

_IOFBF	Used as a third argument to *setvbuf*() indicating that input/output is to be fully buffered.
_IOLBF	Used as a third argument to *setvbuf*() indicating that output is to line buffered.
_IONBF	Used as a third argument to *setvbuf*() indicating that input/output is to be completely unbuffered.
BUFSIZ	The size of the buffer used by *setbuf*().
EOF	A negative constant indicating end-of-file.
L_tmpbuf	The maximum number of characters in a temporary file name generated by *tmpnam*().
OPEN_MAX	The minimum number of files that the implementation guarantees can be open simultaneously.
SEEK_CUR	Used as a third argument to *fseek*() indicating the current file position.
SEEK_END	Used as a third argument to *fseek*() indicating the end-of-file position.
SEEK_SET	Used as a third argument to *fseek*() indicating the beginning of the file.
SYS_OPEN	The minimum number of files that can be open simultaneously.
TMP_MAX	The minimum number of unique file names generated by *tmpnam*().
stderr	A pointer to the standard error file.
stdin	A pointer to the standard input file.
stdout	A pointer to the standard output file.

Figure 9.9 -- Macros in <stdio.h>

9.12.1 Operations on Files

- int remove(const char *filename);
  Remove the file *filename*. If the file is currently open the behaviour is implementation-dependent. Return zero if the named file is successfully removed.

- int rename(const char *old, const char *new);
  Rename the file *old* as *new*. Return zero if the old file is successfully renamed.

- FILE *tmpfile(void);
  Create a temporary binary file and return a pointer to the stream of the file. The file is removed automatically when it is closed. Return *NULL* if the file cannot be created.

- char *tmpnam(char *s);
  Return a pointer to a string that is not the same name as any existing temporary file. If this function is called more than *TMP_MAX* times the behaviour is implementation-dependent. If *s* is not *NULL* it is assumed to point to an array of not less than *L_tmpbuf* characters in which the name is also stored.

9.12.2 File Access Functions

- int fclose(FILE *stream);
  Flush the output buffer of the specified stream and close the associated file. Return zero if successful.

- int fflush(FILE *stream);
  Flush the output buffer of the specified stream. Return non-zero if a write error occurs.

- FILE *fopen(const char *filename, const char *mode);
  Open the file *filename* and associate a stream with it. The access mode is specified by *mode*, which must begin with one of the sequences in Figure 9.10. Return a pointer to the stream if successful.

"r"	Open text file for reading.
"w"	Create text file for writing, or truncate to zero length.
"a"	Append. Open text file or create for writing at end-of-file.
"rb"	Open binary file for reading.
"wb"	Create binary file for writing, or truncate to zero length.
"ab"	Append. Open binary file or create for writing at end-of-file.
"r+"	Open text file for updating (reading and writing).
"w+"	Create text file for update, or truncate to zero length.
"a+"	Append. Open text file or create for update, writing at end-of-file.
"r+b" or "rb+"	Open binary file for update (reading and writing).
"w+b" or "wb+"	Create binary file for update, or truncate to zero length.
"a+b" or "ab+"	Append. Open binary file or create for update, writing at end of file.

Figure 9.10 -- File Opening Modes

- FILE *freopen(const char *filename, const char *mode, FILE *stream);
  Open the file *filename and associate stream with it. The access mode is specified by *mode (see fopen() above).

- void setbuf(FILE *stream, char *buf);
  Equivalent to setvbuf(stream, buf, _IOFBF, BUFSIZ).

112

- int setvbuf(FILE *stream, char *buf, int mode, size_t size);
  The argument *mode* determines how *stream* will be buffered (see Figure 9.9).

9.12.3 Formatted Input/Output Functions

- int fprintf(FILE *stream, const char *format, ...);
  Write output to *stream* under control of the string *format* which specifies how subsequent arguments are converted. The format string contains either plain characters or conversion specifications. A conversion specification has the general form

$$\%fw.pc$$

described in more detail in Figure 9.11.

f	Optional *flag* characters. A minus sign indicates left-justification. A plus sign indicates that a numeric conversion will always be signed.
w	An optional decimal integer indicating a minimum *field-width*. If the integer starts with a zero the padding is with zeros, otherwise with spaces.
p	An optional *precision*.
c	The *conversion* specifier.

Figure 9.11 -- Conversion Specification for fprintf()

The conversion specifiers and their meanings are

c   The *int* argument is converted to an *unsigned char*, and printed.

d   The *int* argument is converted to signed decimal.

e,E The *double* argument is converted to a decimal string of the form [-]d.ddde±dd, where there is one digit before the decimal point and then number of digits after the decimal point is equal to the precision. If the precision is missing, there are six digits after the decimal point. If the precision is zero, the decimal point is omitted.

f   The *double* argument is converted to a decimal string of the form [-]ddd.ddd, where the number of digits after the decimal point is the precision. If the precision is missing, the default value is six. If the precision is zero, the decimal point is omitted. There is always one digit before a decimal point.

g,G The *double* argument is converted in style *f* or *e* (or *E* in the case of *G*), with the precision specifying the number of significant digits.

i   Same as d.

n   The (*int* *) argument is assigned the number of characters written so far by this call to *fprintf*.

o   The *int* argument is converted to unsigned octal.

p   The (*const void* *) argument is converted to a sequence of printable characters in an implementation-dependent manner.

s   The (*const char* *) argument is written as a sequence of characters up to, but not including, the terminating *NUL* character, or until the number of characters indicated by the precision is reached. If the precision is missing, the complete string is written.

u   The *int* argument is converted to unsigned octal.

x,X The *int* argument is converted to unsigned hexadecimal (using *abcdef* for x and *ABCDEF* for X).

%   The character % is written.

   This function returns the number of characters output, or a negative value if an output error occurred. Some examples are given in Figure 9.12 and Figure 9.13. The double-quote characters (") are not output; they are used to indicate the output widths.

%d	"123"	Minimum field width
%10d	" 123"	Right-justified
%010d	"0000000123"	Padded with zeros
%-10d	"123 "	Left-justified
%10o	" 173"	Octal right-justified
%-10x	"7c "	Hexadecimal left-justified

Figure 9.12 -- Integer Output Conversions

%s	"Birkbeck College"	Default field width
%10s	"Birkbeck College"	Minimum field width
%20s	" Birkbeck College"	Right-justified
%-20s	"Birkbeck College "	Left-justified
%.10s	"Birkbeck C"	Precision
%-20.10s	"Birkbeck C "	Left-justified precision

Figure 9.13 -- String Output Conversions

- int fscanf(FILE *stream, const char *format, ...);
  Read input from *stream under control of the string
  *format which specifies how input text is converted for
  assignment to the objects pointed to by subsequent
  arguments. The conversion specification is of the form

                        %*wc

  described in Figure 9.14 and follows the same pattern
  as the specification for fprintf(). Any arguments following the format string must be <u>pointers</u> to objects of
  the appropriate type.

*	An optional assignment-suppressing charac-ter.
w	An optional decimal integer specifying the maximum *field-width*".
c	The *conversion* specifier.

Figure 9.14 -- Conversion Specification for fscanf()

The possible conversion specifiers are

c   A sequence of characters are expected. The number is specified by the field width (default is one).

d   An optionally signed decimal integer is expected.

e   An optionally signed floating-point number is expected.

f   Same as e.

g   Same as e.

i   An optionally signed integer is expected. The format is the same as that of *strtol()* (see Section 9.13.1) with *base* equal to zero.

n   No input takes place. The corresponding argument receives the number of characters read so far by this call.

o   An optionally signed octal integer is expected.

p   A pointer is expected. The interpretation is implementation-dependent, but should correspond with the same argument in *fprintf()*.

s   A character string is expected. The input field is terminated by a space, a horizontal tab, or a newline.

u   An unsigned decimal integer is expected.

x   An optionally signed hexadecimal integer is expected.

[A sequence of specified characters is expected, up to the closing right bracket (]). If the first character is a circumflex (^), then characters <u>not</u> in the set are expected.

%   A single % is expected. No assignment occurs.

This function returns the number of items successfully
matched,   or *EOF* if this is encountered before the first
conversion. For example, the call

```
int ii;
float ff;
char ss[20];
...
        n = fscanf(stdin, "%d%*s%f%s", &ii, &ff, ss);
```

with the input line

123   ignored 45.67E-1 taken

will assign to *n* the value *3*, to *ii* the value *123*, to *ff* the
value *4.567*, and to *ss* the string *"taken"*. Lower case
letters may be added to the conversion specifiers in
fprintf() and *fscanf()*
 in later versions of (stdio.h>.

- `int printf(const char *format, ...);`
  Equivalent to *fprintf(stdout, format, ...)*.

- `int scanf(const char *format, ...);`
  Equivalent to *fscanf(stdin, format, ...)*.

- `int sprintf(char *s, const char *format, ...);`
  Equivalent to *fprintf()* except that the output is written into the string pointed to by *s*.

- `int sscanf(const char *s, const char *format, ...);`
  Equivalent to *fscanf()* except that the input is
  obtained from the string *s*.

- `int vfprintf(FILE *stream, const char *format, va_list
  arg);`
  Equivalent to *fprintf()* except that the variable argument list is replaced by *arg*.

- `int vprintf(const char *format, va_list arg);`
  Equivalent to *printf()* except that the variable argument is replaced by *arg*.

- `int vsprintf(char *s, const char *format, va_list arg);`
  Equivalent to *sprintf()* except that the variable argument list is replaced by *arg*.

9.12.4 Character Input/Output Functions

- int fgetc(FILE *stream);
  Get the next character from the specified stream.
  Return *EOF* if end-of-file or an error is encountered.

- char *fgets(char *s, int n, FILE *stream);
  Read not more than *n-1* characters from *stream* into the
  array pointed to by s, until end-of-file or a newline
  is encountered. Return s if successful or *NULL* if an
  error (or end-of-file) occurs.

- int fputc(int c, FILE *stream);
  Write the character on the specified output stream.
  Return the character written or *EOF* if an error occurs.

- int fputs(const char *s, FILE *stream);
  Write the string *s onto the file *stream. Return zero
  if successful.

- int getc(FILE *stream);
  Equivalent to *fgetc()* except that it may be implemented
  as a macro.

- int getchar(void);
  Equivalent to *getc(stdin)*.

- char *gets(char *s);
  Read characters from *stdin* into the array pointed to by
  s, until end-of-file or a newline is encountered.
  Return s if successful, or *NULL* if an error (or end-
  of-file) occurs.

- int putc(int c, FILE *stream);
  Equivalent to *fputc()* except that it may be implemented
  as a macro.

- int putchar(int c);
  Equivalent to *putc(c, stdout)*.

- int puts(const char *s);
  Write the string onto *stdout* and append a newline.

- int ungetc(int c, FILE *stream);
  Push the character c back onto the specified input
  stream so that it will be returned by the next read on
  that stream.

9.12.5 Direct Input/Output Functions

- size_t fread(void *ptr, size_t size, size_t nmemb, FILE *stream);
  Read not more than *nmemb* objects of size *size* from *stream* into the array pointed to by *ptr*. Return the number of objects read if successful, otherwise zero.

- size_t fwrite(const void *ptr, size_t size, size_t nmemb, FILE *stream);
  Write not more than *nmemb* objects of size *size* from *ptr* onto *stream*. Return the number of objects successfully written.

9.12.6 File Positioning Functions

- int fgetpos(FILE *stream, fpos_t *pos);
  Store the current file position in *pos*. Return zero if successful.

- int fseek(FILE *stream, long offset, int whence); Set the file position indicator for *stream*. For a binary stream the new position is *offset* away from *whence*. This can be *SEEK_CUR*, *SEEK_END*, or *SEEK_SET* as described in Figure 9.9. For a text stream be offset can ftell(). *Ptrname* should be *SEEK_SET*.

- int fsetpos(FILE *stream, const fpos_t *pos);
  Set the file position indicator according to the value of *pos*. It also clears the end-of-file indicator and removes any *unget()* character. Return zero if successful.

- long ftell(FILE *stream);
  Return the current value of the file position indicator for *stream*. For a binary stream this is the number of characters from the beginning of the file. For a text stream the value is implementation-dependent, but usable by *fseek()*.

- void rewind(FILE *stream);
  Equivalent to *fseek(stream, 0L, SEEK_SET)*.

9.12.7 Error-Handling Functions

- void clearerr(FILE *stream);
  Clear the end-of-file and error indicators associated with *stream.

- int feof(FILE *stream);
  Return non-zero if the end-of-file indicator is set for *stream.

- int ferror(FILE *stream);
  Return non-zero if the read/write error indicator is set for *stream.

- void perror(const char *s);
  Map the error number in errno into an error message that is written to the standard error preceded by the string *s and a colon.

9.13 <stdlib.h> – Standard Library

This header declares two types and several functions, and defines four macros.

| div_t | The structure type returned by div. |
| ldiv_t | The structure type returned by ldiv. |

Figure 9.15 -- Types in <stdlib.h>

EDOM	See Figure 9.4.
ERANGE	See Figure 9.4.
HUGE_VAL	See Figure 9.4.
RAND_MAX	The maximum value returned by rand().

Figure 9.16 -- Macros in <stdlib.h>

9.13.1 String Conversion Functions

- double atof(const char *nptr);
  Equivalent to *strtod(nptr, (char **)NULL)*.

- int atoi(const char *nptr);
  Equivalent to *(int)strtol(nptr, (char **)NULL, 10)*.

- long atol(const char *nptr);
  Equivalent to *strtol(nptr, (char **)NULL, 10)*.

- double strtod(const char *nptr, char **endptr);
  Convert the string **nptr* into a *double* value. If *endptr* is not *NULL* a pointer to the terminating charac-ter is stored in **endptr*. This may be *nptr* if the string doesn't start with an appropriate character.

- long strtol(const char *nptr, char **endptr, int base);
  Convert the string **nptr* into a *long* value. If *endptr* is not *NULL* a pointer to the terminating character is stored in **endptr*. If *base* is zero the string is interpreted as an integer constant according to the rules given in Section 1.4.2. If *base* is between two and 36 it is used as the base for conversion. A lead-ing *0x* or *0X* is ignored if the base is 16.

9.13.2 Pseudo-Random Number Functions

- int rand(void);
  Return a pseudo-random integer in the range [0, *RAND_MAX*].

- void srand(unsigned int seed);
  Use the argument as a seed for a new sequence of pseudo-random numbers, returned by *rand()*.

9.13.3 Memory Management Functions

- void *calloc(size_t nmemb, size_t size);
  Allocate space for an array of *nmemb* objects, each of *size* bytes. The space is initialised to all bits zero. *Calloc()* returns a pointer to the start of the space (lowest byte) or *NULL* if the space cannot be allocated or if either *nmemb* or *size* are zero.

- void free(void *ptr);
  Free the space pointed to by *ptr*. If *ptr* is *NULL*, nothing happens, otherwise if the space was not allocated correctly, or has already been de-allocated, the behaviour is undefined.

- void *malloc(size_t size);
  Allocate space for an object of *size* bytes. If the space cannot be allocated, or if *size* is zero, return *NULL*.

- void *realloc(void *ptr, size_t size);
  Change the size of the object pointed to by *ptr* to be *size* bytes.

9.13.4 Environment Communication Functions

- void abort(void);
  Cause the program to terminate abnormally.

- int atexit(void (*func)(void));
  Provide the program with a mechanism to clean up the environment before it exits. Return zero if the registration succeeds. The function pointed to by *func* will be called without arguments at normal program termination.

- void exit(int status);
  Cause the program to terminate normally.

- char *getenv(const char *name);
  Search an implementation-dependent *environment list* for a string of the form *name=value*, and return a pointer to a string matching *value*. If the specified name cannot be found, return *NULL*.

- int system(const char *string);
  Suspend execution of the current program temporarily in order to run another program to completion.

9.13.5 Searching and Sorting Utilities

The two functions in this section take as an argument a pointer to a common comparison function. This function takes two arguments pointing to the objects being compared and returns an integer less than, equal to, or greater than zero if the first object is considered to be less than, equal to, or greater than the second object.

- void bsearch(const void *key, const void *base, size_t nmemb, size_t size, int (*compar)(const void *, const void *));
  Search an array of *nmemb* objects pointed to by *base* for an object matching that pointed to by *key*. Each object is *size* bytes.

- void qsort(void *base, size_t nmemb, size_t size, int (*compar)(const void *, const void *));
  Sort an array of *nmemb* objects pointed to by *base*. Each object is *size* bytes. If two objects are considered equal, their order in the sorted array is undefined.

9.13.6 Integer Arithmetic Functions

- int abs(int j);
  Return the absolute value of *j*.

- div_t div(int numer, int denom);
  Return the quotient and remainder of dividing *numer* by *denom* in a structure of type *div_t*.

- long labs(long j);
  Return the absolute value of *j* as a *long* value.

- ldiv_t ldiv(long numer, long denom);
  Return the quotient and remainder of dividing *numer* by *denom* in a structure of type *ldiv_t*.

9.14 <string.h> – String Handling

This header declares several functions for manipulating strings (arrays of *char*). The goal is to provide equivalent capabilities for three types of byte sequences

str- *NUL*-terminated strings.

strn-*NUL*-terminated strings with a maximum length.

mem- Transparent data of a specified length. These functions are required to work even if the source and destination overlap.

Names beginning with *str* or *mem* are reserved for future use.

9.14.1 Copying Functions

- `void *memcpy(void *s1, const void *s2, size_t n);`
  Copy *n* characters from **s2* into **s1*.

- `char *strcpy(char *s1, const char *s2);`
  Copy the string **s2* into the array **s1*.

- `char *strncpy(char *s1, const char *s2, size_t n);`
  Copy not more than *n* characters from the string **s2* into the array **s1*.

9.14.2 Concatenation Functions

- `char *strcat(char *s1, const char *s2);`
  Append a copy of the string **s2* to the end of the string **s1*.

- `char *strncat(char *s1, const char *s2, size_t n);`
  Append not more than *n* characters of the string **s2* to the end of the string **s1*.

9.14.3 Comparison Functions

These functions return an integer less than, equal to, or greater than zero if the first object is considered to be less than, equal to, or greater than the second object.

- `int memcmp(const void *s1, const void *s2, size_t n);`
  Compare the first *n* characters of the two objects **s1* and **s2*.

- `int strcmp(const char *s1, const char *s2);`
  Compare the two strings **s1* and **s2*.

- `int strncmp(const char *s1, const char *s2, size_t n);`
  Compare not more than *n* characters of the two strings **s1* and **s2*.

124

- `size_t strcoll(char *to, size_t maxsize, const char *from);`
  Transform the string *from* into the string *to* such that two transformed strings can be ordered using *memcmp()* or *strcmp()* according to the program's locale (see Section 9.6). Return the length of the resultant string, otherwise zero.

9.14.4 Search Functions

- `void *memchr(const void *s, int c, size_t n);`
  Locate the first occurrence of *c* in the initial *n* characters of *s*. Return *NULL* if it does not occur.

- `char *strchr(const char *s, int c);`
  Locate the first occurrence of *c* in the string *s*. Return *NULL* if it does not occur.

- `size_t strcspn(const char *s1, const char *s2);`
  Return the length of the initial segment of *s1* containing <u>no</u> characters from *s2*.

- `char *strpbrk(const char *s1, const char *s2);`
  Locate the first occurrence in *s1* of any character from *s2*. Return a pointer to the character, or *NULL* if none exist.

- `char *strrchr(const char *s, int c);`
  Locate the last occurrence of *c* in *s*. Return *NULL* if it does not occur.

- `size_t strspn(const char *s1, const char *s2);`
  Return the length of the initial segment of *s1* consisting entirely of characters from *s2*.

- `char *strstr(const char *s1, const char *s2);`
  Locate the first occurrence of the string *s2* in the string *s1*. Return *NULL* if it does not occur.

- `char *strtok(char *s1, const char *s2);`
  A sequence of calls to *strtok()* partitions *s1* into tokens separated by characters from *s2*. The first call returns a pointer to the first token (if one exists) and overwrites the terminating character with *NUL*. It saves a pointer to the next character. Subsequent calls with a *NULL* first argument scan from this position. This is best illustrated by a short example

```
#include <string.h>
static char passwd[] = "mick::123:45:M.Farmer:";
...
        user = strtok(passwd, ":");
        secret = strtok(NULL, ":");
        uid = strtok(NULL, ":");
        gid = strtok(NULL, ":");
        initial = strtok(NULL, ".");
        surname = strtok(NULL, ":");
```

9.14.5 Miscellaneous Functions

- `void *memset(void *s, int c, size_t n);`
  Copy the value of *c* into the first *n* characters of *s*.

- `char *strerror(int errnum);`
  Return a pointer to an implementation-dependent error message string mapped from *errnum*.

- `size_t strlen(const char *s);`
  Return the length of the string *s*.

9.15 <time.h> – Data and Time

This header defines one macro, three types, and declares several functions for manipulating time. The macro defined is

CLK_TCK

which is the number per second of the value returned by *clock()*.

The types *clock_t* and *time_t* are arithmetic types capable of representing times, and *struct tm* which holds the components of a calendar time, called the *broken-down time*. The minimal members of this structure are given in Figure 9.17.

```
struct tm {
        int tm_sec;        /*seconds after the minute [0-59]*/
        int tm_min;        /*minutes after the hour [0-59]*/
        int tm_hour;       /*hours since midnight [0-23]*/
        int tm_mday;       /*day of the month [1-31]*/
        int tm_mon;        /*month of the year [0-11]*/
        int tm_year;       /*years since 1900*/
        int tm_wday;       /*days since Sunday [0-6]*/
        int tm_yday;       /*day of the year [0-365]*/
        int tm_isdst;      /*daylight saving time flag*/
};
```

Figure 9.17 -- Struct tm

9.15.1 Time Manipulation Functions

* clock_t clock(void);
  Return a good approximation to the processor time used by the program.

* double difftime(time_t time1, time_t time0);
  Return the difference between two calendar times expressed in seconds.

* time_t mktime(struct tm *timeptr);
  Convert the broken-down time, expressed as local time, into a calendar time. If the calendar time cannot be represented the function returns (time_t)-1.

* time_t time(time_t *timer);
  Return a good approximation to the current calendar time.   Return (time_t)-1 if the calendar time is not available.

9.15.2 Time Conversion Functions

* char *asctime(const struct tm *timeptr);
  Return a pointer to a string containing the broken-down time from *timeptr.

* char *ctime(time_t *timer).
  Convert the calendar time in *timer into local time in the form of a string. It is equivalent to

asctime(localtime(timer)).

- struct tm *gmtime(const time_t *timer).
  Convert the calendar time in *timer into a broken-down
  time, expressed as Greenwich Mean Time (GMT).

- struct tm *localtime(const time_t *timer);
  Convert the calendar time in *timer into a broken-down
  time, expressed as local time.

- size_t strftime(char *s, size_t maxsize, const char
  *format, const struct tm *timeptr);
  Put characters into *s under control of the string
  *format, which consists of ordinary characters and
  directives. No more than maxsize characters are put
  into the array. Each directive is replaced by
  appropriate characters according to the list in Figure
  9.18. The appropriate characters are determined by the
  program's locale (see Section 9.6) and the values in
  *timeptr. Return the number of characters put into the
  array.

Directive	Description
%a	The abbreviated weekday name.
%A	The full weekday name.
%b	The abbreviated month name.
%B	The full month name.
%c	The appropriate date and time representation.
%d	The day of the month in decimal [01-31].
%H	The hour (24-hour clock) in decimal [00-23].
%I	The hour (12-hour clock) in decimal [01-12].
%j	The day of the year in decimal [001-366].
%m	The month in decimal [01-12].
%M	The minute in decimal [00-59].
%p	The locale's equivalent of AM or PM.
%S	The second in decimal [00-59].
%U	The week (starting Sunday) number in decimal [00-52].
%w	The weekday in decimal [0-6].
%W	The week (starting Monday) number in decimal [00-52].
%x	The locale's date representation.
%X	The locale's time representation.
%y	The year (within a century) in decimal [00-99].
%Y	The year (with century) in decimal.
%Z	The timezone name.
%%	%.

Figure 9.18 -- Directives for strftime()

Assignment 9.1

The current standard attempts to remove dependencies on
character sets, particular hardware, and operating systems
from the language. However, traces of ASCII, PDP-11, and
UNIX still lurk in the darker recesses, particularly within
the library facilities. Investigate and report on those
found.

Assignment 9.2

Write a function for sorting the employee records of
the NODDY Software Corporation by name. Use the library
function *qsort()* in conjunction with a suitable comparison
function.

Assignment 9.3

Virtually all operating systems used worldwide are
American inventions. Their behaviour and characteristics
reflect the ideas, background, and cultural bias of their
authors. Only 8% of the world's population speak English.
It is therefore important that operating systems and computer languages provide the *international* user with the same
facilities as a *domestic* user. In C, this issue has most
impact on the functions in the various libraries. Major
standards bodies such as ANSI and ISO are looking at ways of
defining and specifying local environments and conventions.
Investigate your local environment. An excellent paper by
Leijonhufvud and Lindgren [46] covers topics such as alphabet, numeric representation, currency representation, and
address format.

Chapter 10
The Cruel C

10.1 Introduction

No one can write perfect programs first time. UNIX provides a number of tools to help the programmer find faults and inefficiencies. This chapter briefly describes those tools of particular interest to the C programmer.

10.2 Lint

One of the basic principles of UNIX is that each tool should perform one job only, and perform it well. *Lint* attempts to find constructions which are (possible) bugs, non-portable, or wasteful. It checks type usage more strictly than the C compilers and reports unreachable statements, loops not entered at the top, and *auto* variables declared and not used. Importantly, it checks the consistency of function arguments and the values returned by functions.

10.3 Adb

Adb is a general purpose debugging program. It is most at home as an assembly level debugger, analysing the core dump of a crashed program, and running the program under debug control. It uses the symbol table from the executable program to display, in many different formats, the contents of the program and the values of variables. Without a symbol table the symbolic features of *adb* cannot be used although the file can still be examined.

10.4 Prof

Prof samples a running program to see which function is running. Using this information a table is printed showing the number of times a function was called and the number of milliseconds per call.

10.5 Cb

Cb is a C program beautifier, sometimes called a "pretty printer". *Cb* reads from the standard input and writes to the standard output so a command like

```
cb <program.c
```

will display a copy of the program with consistent spacing and indentation. The examples in this book have been produced using Kernighan & Ritchie's spacing and indentation conventions ([3], pp.10,16,52) so do not require further beautification.

10.6 Pcc

Pcc is the portable C compiler. It performs the same checks as *lint* as well as being a compiler. In theory, a C program compiled by *pcc* without any errors is portable to other systems.

10.7 Make

UNIX and C are well suited to developing modular programs. Large programs are often composed of a large number of source files with complicated dependencies on header files and system library files. *Make* processes a file containing such dependencies.

Make is not limited to handling C files. The text of this book is maintained using this tool.

10.8 LEX and YACC

LEX and *YACC* are two compiler writing tools. *LEX* accepts regular expressions and associated C fragments corresponding to actions. It is used for lexical analysis, especially of programming languages, and interfaces well with *YACC*.

YACC accepts an LALR(1) grammar and associated C fragments and generates a C program to partition its input according to the grammar. *YACC* expects its input to have been partitioned into tokens by a lexical analyser such as *LEX*.

10.9 And Finally

It is obvious that C is generating a great deal of interest in all fields and disciplines where computers are used. It is being implemented on machines across a very wide spectrum from the smallest microcomputers to the largest super-computers. Traditionally it has been linked with UNIX, but is now available on many different operating systems. C is here to stay.

C++ [38] is an exciting development. It is too early to say whether it will replace "traditional" C as the tool of the software engineer. Definitely something to keep an eye on for the future.

Assignment 10.1

Investigate other languages like C, especially C++ and other system implementation languages.

Assignment 10.2

Create a file, *employee.c*, containing functions for manipulating the employee records of the NODDY Software Corporation. A suitable header file, *employee.h*, should also be created. It should contain your macros defined for Assignment 8.2 and any other useful definitions. The following functions are required:

* *int getperson(FILE *stream, struct person *p);*
  This function reads an unformatted structure from the specified file.†

* *int putperson(FILE *stream, struct person p);*
  This function writes an unformatted (raw) structure to the specified file.

* Your sort function from Assignment 9.2.

  Include other functions that you think necessary.

Assignment 10.3

Rewrite *lint* and *pcc* so that they make use of the information given by function prototypes.

---

†This is the closest C gets to the Pascal concept of a file of records.

Appendix A
The Syntax of C in BNF

```
token:
        keyword
        identifier
        constant
        string-literal
        operator
        punctuator

keyword: one of
        auto      break     case      char      const
        continue            default   do        double
        else      enum      extern    float     for
        goto      if        int       long      register
        return    short     signed    sizeof    static
        struct    switch    typedef   union     unsigned
        void      volatile            while

identifier:
        nondigit
        identifer nondigit
        identifer digit

nondigit: one of
        a         b         c         d         e         f
        g         h         i         j         k         l
        m         n         o         p         q         r
        s         t         u         v         w         x
        y         z         A         B         C         D
        E         F         G         H         I         J
        K         L         M         N         O         P
        Q         R         S         T         U         V
        W         X         Y         Z         _

digit: one of
        0         1         2         3         4         5
        6         7         8         9

constant:
        floating-constant
```

```
            integer-constant
            enumeration-constant
            character-constant

floating-constant:
            fractional-constant exponent-part$_{opt}$
                    floating-suffix$_{opt}$


            digit-sequence exponent-part floating-suffix$_{opt}$




fractional-constant:
            digit-sequence$_{opt}$ . digit-sequence


            digit-sequence .

exponent-part:
            e sign$_{opt}$ digit-sequence


            E sign$_{opt}$ digit-sequence



sign: one of
            +           -

digit-sequence:
            digit
            digit-sequence digit

floating-suffix: one of
            f        l        F        L

integer-constant:
            decimal-constant integer-suffix$_{opt}$
            octal-constant integer-suffix$_{opt}$


            hexadecimal-constant integer-suffix$_{opt}$




decimal-constant:
            nonzero-digit
            decimal-constant digit
```

```
octal-constant:
        0
        octal-constant octal-digit

hexadecimal-constant:
        0x hexadecimal-digit
        0X hexadecimal-digit
        hexadecimal-constant hexadecimal-digit

nonzero-digit: one of
        1         2         3         4         5
        6         7         8         9

octal-digit: one of
        0         1         2         3         4
        5         6         7

hexadecimal-digit: one of
        0         1         2         3         4
        5         6         7         8         9
        a         b         c         d         e
        f         A         B         C         D
        E         F

integer-suffix:
        unsigned-suffix long-suffix_{opt}
        long-suffix unsigned-suffix_{opt}



unsigned-suffix: one of
        u         U

long-suffix: one of
        l         L

enumeration-constant:
        identifier

character-constant:
        ' c-char-sequence '

c-char-sequence:
        c-char
        c-char-sequence c-char

c-char:
        any character in the source character set except
                the single quote ', backslash \, or
                newline character
        escape-sequence
```

escape-sequence: one of
      \'   \"   \?   \\   \o
      \oo   \ooo   \xh   \xhh   \xhhh
      \a   \b   \f   \n   \r
      \t   \v

string-literal:
      " s-char-sequence$_{opt}$ "

s-char-sequence:
      s-char
      s-char-sequence s-char

s-char:
      any character in the source character set except
          the double-quote ", backslash \, or
          newline character
      escape-sequence

operator: one of
      (   )   [   ]   .
      ->   *   &   +   -
      !   ~   ++   --   sizeof
      /   %   <<   >>   <
      >   <=   >=   ==   !=
      ^ | && || ?
      :   =   +=   -=   *=
      /=   %=   >>=   <<=   &=
      ^= |=   ,   #   ##

punctuator: one of
      {   }   (   )   [
      ]   ,   ;   ...   #

primary-expression:
      identifier
      constant
      string-literal
      (expression)

postfix-expression:
      primary-expression
      postfix-expression [expression]
      postfix-expression (argument-expression-list$_{opt}$)

      postfix-expression . identifier
      postfix-expression -> identifier
      postfix-expression ++
      postfix-expression --

argument-expression-list:

```
        assignment-expression
        argument-expression-list , assignment-expression

unary-expression:
        postfix-expression
        ++ unary-expression
        -- unary-expression
        unary-operator cast-expression
        sizeof unary-expression
        sizeof ( type-name )

unary-operator: one of
        &         *         +         -         ~         !

cast-expression:
        unary-expression
        ( type-name ) cast-expression

multiplicative-expression:
        cast-expression
        multiplicative-expression * cast-expression
        multiplicative-expression / cast-expression
        multiplicative-expression % cast-expression

additive-expression:
        multiplicative-expression
        additive-expression + multiplicative-expression
        additive-expression - multiplicative-expression

shift-expression:
        additive-expression
        shift-expression << additive-expression
        shift-expression >> additive-expression

relational-expression:
        shift-expression
        relational-expression < shift-expression
        relational-expression > shift-expression
        relational-expression <= shift-expression
        relational-expression >= shift-expression

equality-expression:
        relational-expression
        equality-expression == relational-expression
        equality-expression != relational-expression

AND-expression:
        equality-expression
        AND-expression & equality-expression

exclusive-OR-expression:
        AND-expression
        exclusive-OR-expression ^ AND-expression
```

```
inclusive-OR-expression:
        exclusive-OR-expression
        inclusive-OR-expression | exclusive-OR-expression

logical-AND-expression:
        inclusive-OR-expression
        logical-AND-expression && inclusive-OR-expression

logical-OR-expression:
        logical-AND-expression
        logical-OR-expression || logical-AND-expression

conditional-expression:
        logical-OR-expression
        logical-OR-expression ? logical-OR-expression
                : conditional-expression

assignment-expression:
        conditional-expression
        unary-expression assignment-operator assignment-express

assignment-operator: one of
        =           +=          -=          *=          /=
        %=          <<=         >>=         &=          ^=
        |=

expression:
        assignment-expression
        expression , assignment-expression

constant-expression:
        conditional-expression

declaration:
        declaration-specifiers init-declarator-list$_{opt}$


declaration-specifiers:
        storage-class-specifier declaration-specifiers$_{opt}$
        type-specifier declaration-specifiers$_{opt}$




init-declarator-list:
        init-declarator
        init-declarator-list , init-declarator

init-declarator:
        declarator
        declarator = initialiser
```

```
storage-class-specifier:
        typedef
        extern
        static
        auto
        register

type-specifier:
        char
        short
        int
        long
        signed
        unsigned
        float
        double
        const
        volatile
        void
        struct-or-union-specifier
        enum-specifier
        typedef-name

struct-or-union-specifier:
        struct-or-union identifier
                { struct-declaration-list }
                                 opt

        struct-or-union identifier

struct-or-union:
        struct
        union

struct-declaration-list:
        struct-declaration
        struct-declaration-list struct-declaration

struct-declaration:
        type-specifier-list struct-declarator-list ;

struct-declarator-list:
        struct-declarator
        struct-declarator-list , struct-declarator

struct-declarator:
        declarator
        declarator    : constant-expression
                  opt

enum-specifier:
        enum identifier   { enumerator-list }
                       opt
```

```
            enum identifier

enumerator-list:
        enumerator
        enumerator-list , enumerator

enumerator:
        enumeration-constant
        enumeration-constant = constant-expression

declarator:
        pointer    direct-declarator
               opt



direct-declarator:
        identifier
        ( declarator )
        direct-declarator [ constant-expression    ]
                                                 opt

        direct-declarator ( parameter-type-list )
        direct-declarator ( identifier-list   )
                                            opt


pointer:
        *  type-specifier-list
                             opt
        *  type-specifier-list   pointer
                             opt


type-specifier-list:
        type-specifier
        type-specifier-list type-specifier

parameter-type-list:
        parameter-list
        parameter-list , ...

identifier-list:
        identifier
        identifier-list , identifier

parameter-list:
        parameter-declaration
        parameter-list , parameter-declaration

parameter-declaration:
        declaration-specifiers declarator
        type-name

type-name:
        type-specifier-list abstract-declarator
                                               opt
```

abstract-declarator:

      pointer
      $pointer_{opt}$ direct-abstract-declarator

direct-abstract-declarator:
      (abstract-declarator)
      $direct\text{-}abstract\text{-}declarator_{opt}$
        [$constant\text{-}expression_{opt}$]

      $direct\text{-}abstract\text{-}declarator_{opt}$
        ($parameter\text{-}type\text{-}list_{opt}$)

typedef-name:
      identifier

initialiser:
      assignment-expression
      { initialiser-list }
      { initialiser-list , }

initialiser-list:
      initialiser
      initialiser-list , initialiser

statement:
      labeled-statement
      compound-statement
      expression-statement
      selection-statement
      iteration-statement
      jump-statement

labeled-statement:
      identifier : statement
      case constant-expression : statement
      default : statement

compound-statement:
      { $declaration\text{-}list_{opt}$ $statement\text{-}list_{opt}$ }

declaration-list:
      declaration
      declaration-list declaration

statement-list:

```
        statement
        statement-list statement

expression-statement:
        expression_opt ;



selection-statement:
        if ( expression ) statement
        if ( expression ) statement else statement
        switch ( expression ) statement

iteration-statement:
        while ( expression ) statement
        do statement while ( expression ) ;
        for ( expression_opt ; expression_opt ; expression_opt )

                statement

jump-statement:
        goto identifier ;
        continue ;
        break ;
        return expression_opt ;



file:
        external-definition
        file external-definition

external-definition:
        function-definition
        declaration

function-definition:
        declaration-specifiers_opt declarator function-body



function-body:
        declaration-list_opt compound-statement
```

Appendix B
Environmental Considerations

B.1 Character Sets

C has traditionally been tied to the ASCII† character set because of its heritage and close links with the UNIX operating system. The current standard has moved away from ASCII despite the precedent of Ada [24] being defined in terms of ASCII. A C implementation has to provide a character set with unique codes for each of the printable graphics and escape sequences. The source character set <u>must</u> provide the 52 upper-case and lower-case letters, the ten decimal digits, and the 29 graphic characters given in Figure B.1.

```
| !    "    #    %    &    ' |
| (    )    *    +    ,    - |
| .    /    :    ;    <    = |
| >    ?    [    \    ]    ^ |
| _    {    |    }    ~      |
|                           |
```

Figure B.1 -- Graphic characters in C

The rationale is that a C implementation must be able to translate a C translator written in C.

B.2 Trigraphs

Trigraphs provide alternative spellings of some of the

†American Standard Code for Information Interchange.

graphics characters. All implementations must support these trigraphs to allow the movement of programs that must use trigraphs. The trigraphs are given in Figure B.2.

??=	#	??(	[	??/	\
??)	]	??'	^	??<	{
??!	|	??>	}	??-	~

Figure B.2 -- Trigraph Sequences

Any other sequence of characters that begins with ?? is unchanged.

B.3 The ASCII Character Set

The ASCII character set is supported by the majority of computer systems. You may find life difficult if yours does not. It is given in Figure B.3.

000 nul	001 soh	002 stx	003 etx
004 eot	005 enq	006 ack	007 bel
010 bs	011 ht	012 nl	013 vt
014 np	015 cr	016 so	017 si
020 dle	021 dc1	022 dc2	023 dc3
024 dc4	025 nak	026 syn	027 etb
030 can	031 em	032 sub	033 esc
034 fs	035 gs	036 rs	037 us
040 sp	041 !	042 "	043 #
044 $	045 %	046 &	047 '
050 (	051)	052 *	053 +
054 ,	055 -	056 .	057 /
060 0	061 1	062 2	063 3
064 4	065 5	066 6	067 7
070 8	071 9	072 :	073 ;
074 <	075 =	076 >	077 ?
100 @	101 A	102 B	103 C
104 D	105 E	106 F	107 G
110 H	111 I	112 J	113 K
114 L	115 M	116 N	117 O
120 P	121 Q	122 R	123 S
124 T	125 U	126 V	127 W
130 X	131 Y	132 Z	133 [
134 \	135]	136 ^	137 _
140 `	141 a	142 b	143 c
144 d	145 e	146 f	147 g
150 h	151 i	152 j	153 k
154 l	155 m	156 n	157 o
160 p	161 q	162 r	163 s
164 t	165 u	166 v	167 w
170 x	171 y	172 z	173 {
174 |	175 }	176 ~	177 del

Apart from printing characters the ASCII character set also defines a number of control characters (the first 32 codes and the last) used in data transmission between computers or between computers and terminals. These are meant to have standard meanings but often differ between systems.

There are seven national characters which can be used for national purposes if required, such as an extended alphabet. However, the majority of computing equipment, most of it originating in the United States, uses the ASCII character set as given above. In the United Kingdom the hash character (#) is sometimes replaced by the pound currency character (£).

Appendix C
UNIX System Calls

This appendix describes the C interface to UNIX. These functions may not be relevant to other operating environments and have therefore been omitted from the standard. Within UNIX these system calls are entries to the kernel. They are the facilities provided by the operating system. Everything else, including the library functions described in Chapter 9, are built on top of them. Full details of the system calls are in Section 2 of the UNIX Programmer's Manual [47]. This chapter describes the most important functions. It is not complete.

- int access(char *name, int mode);
  Check whether file *name is accessible in mode *mode*. Only the access bits are checked.

- int alarm(unsigned seconds);
  Schedule an alarm signal (see Section 9.9 and Figure C.1) after a specified time. Successive calls reset the alarm clock. An argument of zero cancels any alarm request.

- int chdir(char *dirname);
  Change current working directory to the pathname *dirname*.

- int chmod(char *name, int mode);
  Change the mode of file *name* to mode *mode*. Modes are constructed by a combination of the values given in Figure C.1.

04000	Set user-id on execution.
02000	Set group-id on execution.
01000	Save image after execution.
00400	Read by user (owner).
00200	Write by user.
00100	Execute by user.
00040	Read by group.
00020	Write by group.
00010	Execute by group.
00004	Read by others.
00002	Write by others.
00001	Execute by others.

Figure C.1 -- File Modes

- int close(int fildes);
  Close the file associated with the specified file descriptor.

- int creat(char *name, int mode);
  Create a new file or prepare to rewrite an existing file.

- int dup(int fildes);
  Duplicate an open file descriptor synonymous with the original.

- int execl(char *name, char *arg0, ...);
  Overlay the calling process with the named file and execute it. There is no return from a successful *execl*.

- int execv(char *name, char *argv[]);
  One of a number of different flavours of *execl*().

- int fork(void);
  Spawn a new process. The child process is a copy of the parent. The only difference is that the returned value for the parent is the user-id of the child, whereas the returned value for the child is zero. Open

files that are currently open are shared. This is how
pipes are set up.

Example C.1

In this example the current process creates a child
process and waits for it to complete. Since only one child
is created the test on line 10 is redundant. However, it
demonstrates how the shell creates a sub-process in order to
execute a command.

```
 1 /*fork.c*/
 2 #include <stdio.h>
 3 int main(void)
 4 {
 5     int child;
 6     if(child = fork()) {
 7         int status;
 8         int w = wait(&status);
 9         printf("I'm the parent\n");
10         if(child == w)
11             printf("Child status = %d\n", status);
12         else
13             printf("Wait error = %d\n", w);
14     } else {
15         printf("I'm the child\n");
16     }
17     exit(0);
18 }
```

- int getegid(void);
  Return the effective group-id.

- int geteuid(void);
  Return the effective user-id.

- int getgid(void);
  Return the real group-id of the current process.

- int getpid(void);
  Return the process-id of the current process. This is
  always unique.

- int getuid(void);
  Return the real user-id of the current process.

- int ioctl(int fildes, int request, struct sgttyb
  *argp);
  Control a device. There a zillions of options ([17],

pp.286-289).

- int kill(int pid, int sig)
  Send the signal *sig* to the process, or group of processes, associated with the process id *pid*.

(1) If *pid* is zero, the signal is sent to all processes, excluding 0 and 1, whose process group id is equal to the process group of the sender.

(2) If *pid* is -1, the signal is sent to all processes with that user id.

(3) If *pid* is negative, but not -1, the signal is sent to all processes whose group id is equal to the absolute value of *pid*.

Kill() returns zero if successful. The signals and their values on a Version 7 UNIX system are given in Figure C.2.

151

1	SIGHUP	Hangup.
2	SIGINT	Interrupt. Either *del* or *break* from the keyboard.
3	SIGQUIT	Quit. Usually *fs* from the keyboard.
4	SIGILL	Illegal instruction.
5	SIGTRAP	Trace trap or breakpoint. Used by *adb*.
6	SIGIOT	IOT Instruction. Used by *adb*.
7	SIGEMT	EMT instruction. Used on machines without floating-point hardware.
8	SIGFPE	Floating point exception. Usually a divide by zero or an operation resulting in overflow.
9	SIGKILL	Kill. This signal cannot be caught or ignored.
10	SIGBUS	Bus error. Usually caused by an illegal pointer reference.
11	SIGSEGV	Segmentation violation. This is often caused by an invalid access to a data object.
12	SIGSYS	Bad system call.
13	SIGPIPE	End of pipe. This occurs when the process on the receiving end of a pipe terminates.
14	SIGALRM	Alarm clock. This is generated by *pause()*.
15	SIGTERM	Software termination. This is the default signal for the *kill* command and allows processes to terminate gracefully.

Figure C.2 -- UNIX Version 7 <signal.h>

- int link(char *name1, char *name2);
  A link to *name1 is created with the name *name2.
  Either name may be an arbitrary path name.

- long lseek(int fildes, long offset, int whence);
  Move the read/write pointer.

- int nice(int incr);
  Set the process's priority.

- int open(char *name, int mode);
  Open the named file for reading or writing.

- void pause(void);
  Stop until a signal occurs. There is no return.

- int pipe(int fildes[2]);
  UNIX users are familiar with the use of pipes to feed
  the standard output from one program into the standard
  input of another. For example, the string

                         who | sort

  tells the shell to create a pipe between the output of
  who and the input of sort. Programs using a pipe run
  concurrently, not sequentially. Kernighan & Plauger
  ([48], p.126) give a slightly different version of

          cat ... | tr A-Z a-z | tr ^a-z \n | sort -u
          | comm -2 dictionary

  for implementing a spelling checker!

Example C.2

This example reads and writes a number of blocks using
a pipe. It can be used to compare the efficiency of pipe
input/output with that of file input/output.

```
1 /*pipecopy.c*/
2 #include <stdlib.h>
3 #define BLOCK 512
4 char buffer[BLOCK];
5 int main(int argc, char *argv[])
6 {
7     int n = atoi(argv[1]);
8     int fd[2];
9     pipe(fd);
```

```
10        while(n--) {
11             write(fd[1], buffer, BLOCK);
12             read(fd[0], buffer, BLOCK);
13        }
14 }
```

- int read(int fildes, char *buffer, int nbytes);
  Read *nbytes* bytes into *buffer* from the specified file.

- int setgid(int gid);
  Set the effective group-id.

- int setuid(int uid);
  Set the effective user-id.

- int umask(int complmode);
  Set a file creation mode mask.

- int unlink(char *name);
  Remove the directory entry for the named file.

- int wait(int *status);
  Wait for a child process to terminate. See Example C.1.

- int write(int fildes, char *buffer, int nbytes);
  Write *nbytes* bytes from *buffer* to the specified file.

References

1. Henry Wadsworth Longfellow, *The Secret of the Sea*.

2. American National Standards Committee, *Draft Proposed American National Standard For Information Systems -- Programming Language C*, X3J11/86-151, October 1, 1986.

3. Brian W. Kernighan and Dennis M. Ritchie, *The C Programming Language*, Prentice-Hall, Inc., Englewood Cliffs, New Jersey (1978). ISBN 0-13-110163-3

4. Martin Richards, "BCPL: A Tool for Compiler Writing and Systems Programming", *Proc. AFIPS SJCC*, pp.557-566 (1969).

5. Christopher Strachey and J.E. Stoy, "OS6 -- An experimental operating system for a small computer", *Computer Journal* Vol. **15**, pp.117-124, 195-203 (1972).

6. S.C. Johnson and Brian W. Kernighan, "The Programming Language B", *Comp. Sci. Tech. Rep.*(8) (January 1973).

7. A. van Wijngaarden, "Revised Report on the Algorithmic Language ALGOL 68", Technical Report TR74-3, Department of Computing Science, The University of Alberta, Edmonton, Alberta (D).

8. K. Jensen and Niklaus Wirth, *PASCAL User Manual and Report (2nd edition)*, Springer-Verlag, New York (1978). ISBN 0-387-90144-2

9. *Hisoft C*, Hi-Soft, Dunstable, Bedfordshire.

10. Cray Research, Inc., *Cray C Compiler Reference Manual (Release 1)*, SR2024, March, 1986.

11. Harvey J. Hindin, "Improved C compilers boost system throughput.", *Computer Design*, pp.54-61 (September, 1986).

12. American Accredited Standards Committee, *Rationale for Draft Proposed American National Standard for Information Systems -- Programming Language C*, X3J11/86-152, October 1, 1986.

13. Al Kelley and Ira Pohl, *A Book on C*, The Benjamin/Cummings Publishing Company, Inc., Menlo Park, California 94025 (1984). ISBN 0-8053-6860-4

14. Leendert Ammeraal, *C for Programmers*, John Wiley and Sons Ltd., Chichester (1986). ISBN 0-471-91128-3

15. Douglas J. Brown, *From Pascal to C*, Wadsworth Publishing Company, Belmont, California 94002 (1985). ISBN 0-534-04602-9

16. Jon R. Malone, *Comparative Languages*, Chartwell-Bratt Ltd., Bromley, Kent (1984). ISBN 0-86238-067-7

17. S.R. Bourne, *The UNIX System*, Addison-Wesley Publishing Company, Inc., London (1982). ISBN 0-201-13791-7

18. Dennis M. Ritchie, "A Retrospective", *The Bell System Technical Journal* Vol. 57(6), pp.1947-1969, ISSN 0005-8580 (July-August, 1978).

19. Thomas Plum, *C Programming Guidelines*, Prentice-Hall, Inc., Englewood Cliffs, New Jersey (1984). ISBN 0-13-109992-2

20. Televideo Systems, Inc., *Televideo Model 925 CRT Terminal Installation and User's Guide*, Televideo Systems, Inc., Sunnyvale, California 94086 (1982).

21. M.R.M. Dunsmuir and G.J. Davies, *Programming the UNIX System*, Macmillan Publishers Ltd., Basingstoke, Hampshire (1985). ISBM 0-333-37156-9

22. Brian Hayes, "Computer Recreations -- On the ups and downs of hailstone numbers", *Scientific American* Vol. 250(1), pp.13-17 (January, 1984).

23. Harvey M. Deitel, *An Introduction to Operating Systems*, Addison-Wesley Publishing Company, Inc., Reading, Massachusetts (1984). ISBN 0-201-14502-2

24. J.G.P. Barnes, *Programming in Ada*, Addison-Wesley Publishing Company, Inc., London (1982). ISBN 0-201-13793-3, ISBN 0-201-13792-5 (pbk.)

25. Mick Farmer, *The Intensive Pascal Course*, Chartwell-Bratt Ltd., Bromley, Kent (1984). ISBN 0-86238-063-4

26. Kenneth E. Iverson, *A Programming Language*, John Wiley and Sons, Inc., New York (1962).

27. R.M. Burstall, J.S. Collins, and R.J. Popplestone, *Programming in POP-2*, Edinburgh University Press, Edinburgh (1971). ISBN 0-85224-197-6

28. Donald E. Knuth, *The Art of Computer Programming (Volume 2 -- Seminumerical Algorithms)*, Addison-Wesley Publishing Company, Reading, Massachusetts (1969).

29. *A Network Independent File Transfer Protocol*, File Transfer Protocol Implementors Group, Teddington, Middlesex (5 February, 1981). FTP-B(80)

30. *American National Standard Programming Language FORTRAN*, American National Standards Institute, Inc., New York (1978).

31. Donald E. Knuth, *The Art of Computer Programming (Volume 3 -- Sorting and Searching)*, Addison-Wesley Publishing Company, Reading, Massachusetts (1973).

32. Edsgar W. Dijkstra, "Go To Statement Considered Harmful", *Comm. ACM* Vol. **11**(3), pp.147-148 (March, 1968).

33. H.W. Turnbull, *Theory of Equations*, Oliver and Boyd, Edinburgh (1947).

34. William A. Wulf, Mary Shaw, Paul N. Hilfinger, and Lawrence Flon, *Fundamental Structures of Computer Science*, Addison-Wesley Publishing Company, Inc., Reading, Massachusetts (1981). ISBN 0-201-08725-1

35. J.S. Rohl, *Recursion via Pascal*, Cambridge University Press, Cambridge (1984). ISBN 0-521-26329-8 (hardback), ISBN 0-521-26934-2 (paperback)

36. Lawrie Moore, *Foundations of Programming with Pascal*, Ellis Horwood Ltd., Chichester, Sussex (1980). ISBN 0-85312-171-0

37. Donald E. Knuth, *The Art of Computer Programming (Volume 1 -- Fundamental Algorithms)*, Addison-Wesley Publishing Company, Reading, Massachusetts (1968).

38. Bjarne Stroustrup, *The C++ Programming Language*, Addison-Wesley Publishing Company, Inc., Reading, Massachusetts (1985). ISBN 0-201-12078-X

39. Robert T. Gregory and David L. Karney, *A Collection of Matrices for Testing Computational Algorithms*, John Wiley & Sons, Inc., New York (1969). SBN 471-32669-0

40. "How to use this Guide", in *The Good Food Guide*, ed. Drew Smith, Consumers' Association, London (1986). ISBN 0-340-38157-4

41. Peter J. Brown, "Macro Processors", pp. 89-98 in *Software Portability*, ed. Peter J. Brown, Cambridge University Press, Cambridge (1977). ISBN 0-521-21485-8

42. Christopher Strachey, "A General Purpose Macrogenerator", *Computer Journal* Vol. **8**(3), pp.225-241 (1965).

43. Peter J. Brown, "The ML/1 Macro Processor", *Comm. ACM* Vol. **10**(10), pp.618-623 (1967).

44. Brian W. Kernighan and Dennis M. Ritchie, "The M4 Macro Processor", in *UNIX TIME-SHARING SYSTEM: UNIX PROGRAMMER'S MANUAL*, Bell Telephone Laboratories, Inc., Murray Hill, New Jersey 07974 (July, 1977).

45. Richard H. Eckhouse, *Minicomputer Systems: Organization and Programming (PDP-11)*, Prentice-Hall, Inc., Englewood Cliffs, New Jersey (1975). ISBN 0-13-583906-8

46. Greger K. Leijonhunfvud and Gary L. Lindgren, *An Overview of Internationalisation*, IEEE P1003.1 (POSIX Working Group) (September, 1986). C.29

47. Brian W. Kernighan and Dennis M. Ritchie, "UNIX Programming -- Second Edition", in *UNIX TIME-SHARING SYSTEM: UNIX PROGRAMMER'S MANUAL*, Bell Laboratories, Murray Hill, New Jersey 07974 (November 12, 1978).

48. Brian W. Kernighan and P.J. Plauger, *Software Tools*, Addison-Wesley Publishing Company, Reading, Massachusetts (1976). ISBN 0-201-03669-X

Index

167